Homeless Shelter Design

Considerations for Shaping Shelters
and the Public Realm

John R. Graham
Christine A. Walsh
Beverly A. Sandalack

Dedication

This book is dedicated to the memory
of Nicholas "Nick" Hunter Morgan

Homeless Shelter Design:
Considerations for Shaping Shelters and the Public Realm
© 2008 John R. Graham, Christine A. Walsh, Beverly A. Sandalack

Library and Archives Canada Cataloguing in Publication

Graham, John R. (John Russell), 1964-
     Homeless shelter design : considerations for shaping shelters and the public
realm / John R. Graham, Christine A. Walsh, and Beverly A. Sandalack.

Includes bibliographical references.
ISBN 978-1-55059-357-0

     1. Shelters for the homeless--Design. 2. Shelters for the homeless--Location. 3.
City planning. 4. Homelessness. I. Walsh, Christine Ann II. Sandalack, Beverly A.
(Beverly Ann), 1953- III. Title.

HD7287.95.G73 2008   363.5   C2008-905938-7

Detselig Enterprises Ltd.

210, 1220 Kensington Road NW
Calgary, Alberta T2N 3P5
www.temerondetselig.com
Phone: (403) 283-0900   Fax: (403) 283-6947

We acknowledge the support of the Government of Canada through the Book
Publishing Industry Development Program (BPIDP) for our publishing program.

We also acknowledge the support
of the Alberta Foundation for the
Arts for our publishing program.

COMMITTED TO THE DEVELOPMENT OF CULTURE AND THE ARTS

SAN 113-0234
ISBN 978-1-55059-357-0
Cover Design by Francisco Alaniz Uribe

Contents

Acknowledgments

The authors gratefully acknowledge the financial support of the Torode Foundation, the Social Science and Humanities Research Council, and the People and Place Initiative (University of Calgary, City of Calgary). We are indebted to the myriad informants and shelter personnel who have been unfailingly helpful in the research of this book. Sincere thanks are likewise extended to Faculty of Social Work students Michael Shier, Elizabeth Austrum, Sarah Bromley-Meagher, Jenine Hamonic, Nikoo Najand, Alexandra Sears, and Annika Spence, and Faculty of Environmental Design students Braden Abrams Reid, Francisco Alaniz Uribe, Fraser Blyth, and Matt Knapik for invaluable research assistantship. We would also like to express our appreciation to Anda Avens and Erinn Wanek-Walsh who took many photographs.

Authors' Biographies

John R. Graham is Murray Fraser Professor of Community Economic Development at the Faculty of Social Work, University of Calgary, and the Faculty's PhD Program Coordinator. He has published nine books, over sixty-five journal articles and over forty book chapters on social services in Canada and in the Arab Middle East as well as on Canadian social policy. His co-authored *Canadian Social Policy: An Introduction* recently appeared in third edition, and his co-authored *Helping Professional Practice with Indigenous Peoples: The Bedouin-Arab Case* appears in 2008. A former psychiatric social worker, Graham has over twenty years of experience in the social services as a practitioner and scholar.

Christine A. Walsh is an Associate Professor, Faculty of Social Work, University of Calgary and an Adjunct Professor, School of Social Work, McMaster University. Her research interests include contributing to the understanding of violence across the lifespan and the experiences of oppressed or marginalized populations, including those affected by poverty and homelessness. She has published over forty journal papers and four book chapters.

Beverly A. Sandalack is Professor and founding Coordinator of the Urban Design Program at the University of Calgary, and Director of The Urban Lab, a research group in the Faculty of Environmental Design. She is principal of Sandalack & Associates, a Calgary firm specialized in urban design, small town and neighborhood planning, and design and open space planning. Her work with the Urban Lab and her professional work has received local, national, and international awards. She is co-author of *The Calgary Project: Urban Form/Urban Life*, published in 2006. Bev is a Fellow of the Canadian Society of Landscape Architecture, Past President of the Alberta Association of Landscape Architects, Chair of Competitions of the International Federation of Landscape Architects, Charter Member and Deputy Chair of Calgary's Urban Design Review Panel, member of the Canadian Institute of Planners, and is a frequently invited speaker at local, national and international conferences.

Chapter 1

Introduction

Design contributes to how we see our cities and, through its connection with function, it determines how we live within our cities. This book provides insight into one aspect of this interconnection: the design and function of shelters for homeless individuals. It evolved out of an applied research project – a fusion between the disciplines of environmental design and social work – that sought to better appreciate design possibilities for a homeless shelter in downtown Calgary, Alberta, Canada. Our initial intention was to understand one Calgary shelter, and various options of redevelopment and expansion that its administrators might consider. But through a deeper analysis, a broader story emerged. We found little scholarship on the question of how to design and plan shelters for homeless people. And the research we undertook for this project – analyzing potential principles of design for sixty-three shelters in twenty-five cities in three countries – struck us as relevant beyond the immediate city of Calgary. We began the research process for this book by interviewing over fifty key informants who had international reputations in the operation or design of shelters for the homeless. Based on these conversations, as well as extensive reading, we visited shelters for homeless people throughout the world, interviewing staff and the people who used shelter services. Through those contacts, we found further shelters we could examine. The principles that began to emerge were not only useful to our work in Calgary, but also, we concluded, could be helpful to people interested in the design of shelters for the homeless in general. And so the book studies the design considerations of one particular shelter in Calgary from our precedent research within and beyond the city of Calgary. These two things – the specifics as to Calgary and the more general principles that emerge in relation to Calgary and those precedents beyond it – are the main subject matter of this book.

This book is divided into four chapters. The remainder of this chapter considers the notion of home and homelessness in greater detail, and it provides a discussion of homelessness and shelter service delivery within its social context. This brief introduction to homelessness, homeless shelters, and the link between homeless shelters and broader communities creates a context for the remainder of the book. Chapter Two provides an overview of urban planning and design, particularly as they relate to the inclusion of homeless individuals within this discipline. The latter part of Chapter Two presents a spatial analysis of the Mustard Seed Street Ministry (the Calgary shelter that is the local context for this research). Chapter Three describes the precedent research conducted that focuses on specific characteristics of the physical realm and the subsequent implications on community integration of shelter services, based on our analysis of the sixty shelter visits and fifty key informant interviews in several countries. The final chapter identifies design and service delivery recommendations proposed for the Mustard Seed Street Ministry and discusses the applicability of the research for other shelters, mostly in advanced industrialized nations in North America and Europe.

Our research examines the exteriors of homeless shelters only; shelter interiors are equally worthy of research but are beyond the scope of this book. Shelters for homeless people are a regrettable phenomenon, but they do comprise our society's current response to the reality of homelessness. In an ideal world, there would be no homelessness; all citizens would be adequately housed. The Universal Declaration of Human Rights (1948) of the United Nation clearly states the necessity of shelter for all people:

Everyone has the right to a standard of living adequate for the health and well-being of himself and of his family, including food, clothing, housing and medical care and necessary social services, and the right to security in the event of unemployment, sickness, disability, widowhood, old age or other lack of livelihood in circumstances beyond his control. (article 25, para. 1)

It is lamentable that within the sixty years since this declaration was proposed, and in such a prosperous nation as Canada, this right continues to be denied to its citizens.

And so the following pages are written with profound regret: regret for the fact that there are homeless people in Canada, other advanced industrialized nations like it, and indeed throughout the world. And regret that there is a need for our book – which considers how homeless shelters might be planned and designed more humanely. We hope that the future will be better than the present, and that one day, homeless shelters will be no more, consigned to the distant recollections of history.

Home and Homelessness in Context

Life requires certain things. There are substances that sustain us – including food and water. But the physical world can be harsh, and so we seek shelter from the elements and thereby avoid harm from the heat, cold, or violent storms. We are social beings too; we need each other in families and communities. Families provide the structure in which young are born and develop to adulthood; they allow parents to find mutual help and comfort; they nurture the development of individual and collective potentials, meanings, and identities. In our communities, homes are the desired structures in which these things occur: where we experience the physical, psychological, social, and emotional security that we need to thrive. In the best instances too, home is a place of belonging, where some of the most vital relationships take hold and are strengthened (Lasch, 1975; Rybczynski, 1987; Werner, 1987) and the daily routines of home life reinforce these components (Sixsmith, 1986; Taylor & Brower, 1985). Home is of central importance to individuals and their primary relationships (Renshaw, 2007). It is reasonable to conclude that good family-home environments provide essential support for individuals, and it is not surprising that those who perceive that they have such supports are less likely to have mental health problems than those who do not (Turagabeci, Nakamura, Kizuki, & Takano, 2007). A lack of a home may preclude the opportunity to build adequate supporting relationships, and various others of life's essential resources. The stability of having a home can mean the difference between life and death, illness or health. Homes determine so many things. Even the status of owning versus renting has a significant impact on an individual's health, wellbeing, and mortality (Laaksonen, Martikainen, Nihtilä, Rahkoene, & Lahelma, 2008). A home is both a physical structure – with walls and a floor, a roof and a door – and a social structure. It is not just where your house is; it is "wherever," as essayist Christian Morgenstern (1918) puts it, "we are understood."

Appreciated in this light, it is therefore not grandiose to claim that homes are the major medium in which modern history has unfolded. And like all things, homes have evolved. Prior to the Industrial Revolution, the home was hardly, as it is currently in Canada, a private haven from the hustle and bustle of everyday social intercourse or a place where just family members cohabit (Despres, 1991). In part for financial reasons, but largely because it was a common convention, many mid-nineteenth-century Canadian households – even those run by the well-to-do – contained boarders not necessarily connected to the family by birth or prior friendship (Katz, 1975). In addition, upper class families generally had a number of servants, while middle class households had at least one to render cooking, cleaning, gardening, and other functions that were necessary for daily living (Hareven, 1991). Homes often produced clothing and food for familial consumption, and many families also sold these domestically produced items outside of the home (Taylor & Brower, 1985). The pre-industrial home was also a social and spiritual focal point. In contemporary Canada, key developmental milestones such as birth, marriage ceremonies, dying, and funeral rites occur outside of the home. In the past, however, they took place within it. Similarly, almost all recreational activities – reading, socializing with family members or friends, dancing, producing music, and so on – frequently happened at home (Hayden, 1982; Hill, 1985). With the exception of a very small minority of people who could afford outside, institutional instruction, the home also provided educational instruction for youth (Tognoli & Howritz, 1982). It was also a common locus of care for family members who could not as adults fend for themselves due to sickness, old age, or other causes of unemployment (Wright, 1980).

Throughout North America and Western Europe, industrialization changed these practices. The new norm became employment outside the home rather than within it. Mass production of consumer goods also allowed people to purchase food and other amenities outside the home. The need for servants fell; the conventions of having borders gradually dissipated. As a result, the home became a place for members usually just of the nuclear family. And it evolved into a refuge from urban life – a haven that, as Carol Gilman noted in a 1903 primer, "offered rest, peace, quiet, comfort, health and personal expression" (as cited in Saunders & Williams, 1988, p. 82). The post-World War II period consummated an era of suburban housing, building upon that century's earlier garden city movement, with the latter's small communities adjacent to major urban centres. By then, despite remaining a resource-based economy, Canada had ceased to be a rural society. In 1922, for the first time in Canadian history, more than half of all its citizens lived in urban or suburban settings, and by 1950 it was sixty-two percent (Statistics Canada, 2005). In 2006, the most recent year for which data is available, that proportion has increased to eighty percent (Statistics Canada, 2008).

Just as housing has its own meaning and history, so too does homelessness. In the past, as now, some individuals who could not care for themselves and were without family to provide assistance – orphans, the elderly, the sick, the infirm, the mentally ill, or delinquents – might have been provided accommodation within the households of others. But other institutions emerged to help people who had no comparable community supports. In England, Elizabethan Poor Law traditions distinguished between the deserving and undeserving poor. The able bodied poor were given outdoor or indoor work for a low wage. Those who were too young, old, or ill to work would be looked after in almshouses, hospitals, orphanages, or poor houses. Those who were deemed idle – capable but unmotivated to work – received no supports and potential public condemnation (Rothman, 1971). For centuries, privately run, publicly sanctioned debtors' prisons were common. People could languish for years is such prisons. His father's incarceration in a debtor's prison provided Charles Dickens with the lifelong commitment to social betterment, providing the inspiration for many of his progressive books that so greatly influenced Victorian opinion.

This overall approach came to Canada in colonial times. New France saw the emergence of hospitals and various charitable orders that followed a Roman Catholic eleemosynary (charity) tradition. From the late eighteenth century there were poor laws, and ultimately poor law commissioners in provinces such as New Brunswick. From the mid-nineteenth century, Houses of Industry were built in major cities such as Toronto, Ontario. There, outdoor and indoor relief occurred, and affordable housing for the infirmed elderly was also provided (Graham, Swift, & Delaney, 2008).

The transformation away from this particular system of social welfare to a modern one was gradual, with piecemeal labor, income security, and other social welfare legislation: in 1872 trade unions were legalized and by

1890 there were approximately 240 unions nationwide. In the latter half of the nineteenth century, public education had come into its own. And in the early twentieth century, the governments introduced various income security programs which were intended to help keep people out of the poverty that often leads to homelessness: Workers' Compensation (first in Ontario, 1914), Mothers' Allowances (first in Manitoba, 1916), Old Age Security (originally a selective program, co-financed by provincial and federal governments, 1927), among others. Great Depression of the 1930s precipitated major federal government policies culminating in the 1943 Marsh Report, a blueprint for the postwar welfare state. Major federal-level income security programs followed: unemployment insurance (1941), universal Old Age Security (1951), and the Canada Pension Plan (1966). A universal health insurance (mid-1960s to early 1970s) and the Canada Assistance Plan (1966) provided federal government funding for the provincial delivery of health, income security, and universal primary and secondary education (Graham, Swift, & Delaney, 2008). The 1950s and 1960s were a period of buoyant optimism, and social policy analysts saw poverty as a social problem that could be resolved (Galbraith, 1958).

But the mid-1970s to the present era have ushered in a newer, and in our view, less hopeful period of social policy (Graham, 1995). The federal government started to incrementally diminish transfers to provinces in the mid-1970s, and further reductions would occur over the next thirty-five years. Federal income security programs such as Employment Insurance and Workers' Compensation, and provincial income security programs for the disabled and unemployed, were decreased in scope, comprehensiveness, and entitlement. Universal programs such as Family Allowances were eliminated (1944-1992). Others, such as Old Age Security, ceased to be universal because of income tax clawbacks beginning in 1989. Cuts to all areas of social welfare and across all three levels of government – from health delivery to corrections – had a negative impact on those factors that put people at risk of being poor, vulnerable, and homeless. Food banks first emerged in the early 1980s, and increasing numbers of homeless have been observed now for over thirty years (Graham, Swift, & Delaney, 2008).

Those institutions that used to care for those at risk of homelessness – such as psychiatric hospitals – were often very overcrowded dreadful places to be, and were even dumping grounds for orphaned children in some provinces such as Quebec (Riga, 2008). In an effort to render them more humane, psychiatric practice had adopted in the 1960s an explicit mandate to encourage community reintegration. But where would discharged psychiatric patients live within the broader community? Historically, many low income and marginally employed single people found housing in large boarding homes and single room occupancy hotel rooms. Sometimes these were located on a city's *skid row*. Post-World War Two urban renewal swept many of these low cost options away. "Slum clearance" was to make way for large-scale social housing projects, and so came the era of publicly funded housing in high-density contexts. Regent Park in Toronto exemplifies the social housing high rises that graced many North American urban skylines at that time (Rose, 1958). During this same period, the practice of letting out low-cost rooms was increasingly restricted by municipal legislation. Boarding homes and low cost hotels – the typical place that prevented homelessness among itinerant men – were no longer readily available. Homelessness did not emerge solely because of a shortage of adequate shelter, but, rather, due to a number of factors. One of them included a societal shift in the constructed norms of family life that made access to low-cost, single-occupant shelter increasingly difficult (Shlay & Rossi, 1992).

Defining Homelessness

There are myriad definitions of homelessness. One of the best describes homelessness in both practical and literal terms, based on the physical conditions in which individuals negotiate shelter (Fitzpatrick, Kemp, & Klinker, 2000):

- not sleeping/living under a roof.
- living in a homeless shelter facility or similar institutional setting.
- staying in these institutions for extended periods of time because there is no other accommodating situation.
- residing in places that are not long-term solutions to homelessness: Staying with friends or *squatting*, taking up residence illegally in an abandoned building or using land illegally to build shelter.
- living in conditions that would be considered intolerable and/or sharing space with other people in an involuntary capacity. (Kleniewski, 2002)

The following pages focus on those individuals without shelter who are accessing shelter services. The reason for this is obvious: shelter support is a common intervention for those experiencing homelessness. We also recommend various improvements regarding how this support is provided, and hope that we may modestly influence more humane, less stigmatizing services for people experiencing homelessness.

Present Social Context of Homelessness

One obvious thing that unites *homeless* as an analytical category is the common lack of personalized shelter or home. But as previous pages have insisted, it is a mistake to think of the homeless as a single homogenous entity; there are such complex factors inextricably linked with homelessness: mental illness, disability, addiction, history of family violence, marital dissolution, unemployment, educational needs, and the various systemic factors to do with policy and government and economic conditions. A common issue homeless people encounter, though, is stigma and discrimination from the broader community. Some common perceptions of the homeless that some people hold are that they are dangerous, lazy, have poor personal hygiene, or are dishonest (Hocking & Lawrence, 2000; Fink & Tasman, 1992). In fact such negative perceptions are both created and perpetuated by a broader community's lack of attention to the true factors that create homelessness. The homeless may be marginalized both economically and socially; many are victims of theft, physical and sexual assault, and drug-dealers; some are equipped with minimal coping skills and support structures. Homeless individuals as a category are perhaps the most vulnerable members of any city. Being homeless may also deeply influence one's sense of self. The sheer time and energy taken up with survival often turns homelessness into the defining attribute of one's existence (Anderson, 1998). It is therefore important to alter the internalization of homelessness and work toward implementing improved conceptions of self and potential. But this is difficult, if not impossible if homeless people remain socially isolated and unsupported by the community. Homeless shelter management can actively facilitate self-determination in their clientele through service models that promote collaboration around rules and expectations and support client dignity, such as shelters providing single rooms rather than dormitory-style accommodations. The positive implications of these methods of service delivery have been documented within the literature. They do not take into account, though, the relationship between service delivery and urban planning and, specifically, the built environment. The literature is missing an assessment of the social context of the physical realm within our cities and our local communities.

Ethnographic research has identified the development of a homeless subculture amongst some who are experiencing homelessness (Snow & Anderson, 1993; Wagner, 1993; Winchester & Costello, 1995). Such subcultures are in part a response to the social polarization between homeless and non-homeless people due to stigma; a division that may limit the ability for cohabitation of these two groups in an organized civil society (Taylor, 1996). Sennett (1969) long ago pointed out that social clustering within cities can result. Persons of homogenous status and needs unwittingly drift into, consciously select, or are forced by circumstance into the same area. Situating homeless shelters in already marginalized areas perpetuates the stigma that homeless people face and reinforces the message that homeless people do not belong in other neighborhoods. Geography plays a considerable role in determining opportunity structures, and this has a very real impact on the production of inequality within a region (Lobao, Hooks, & Tickamyer, 2007). Further, different parts of a city maintain specialized functions. Consequently, the city may come to resemble a mosaic of social worlds in which the transition from one to the other may be abrupt and interaction between diverse communities can be limited. Understanding the social context of the physical realm in such a manner requires an appraisal of the physical factors impacting the further marginalization of people who experience homelessness.

Causes and Prevention of Homelessness

Poverty, and therefore homelessness, affects the most vulnerable people in capitalist societies; these groups include children, women, persons with disabilities, new immigrants, ethnic minorities, Aboriginal people, and seniors. Regarding women, institutional forms of discrimination in the form of gendered income disparities (a wage gap between genders) and "lack of an effective national child-care program" (Wallis & Kwok, 2008, p. 11) both contribute to poverty and susceptibility to homelessness. According to Wallis and Kwok (2008), nineteen percent of adult women in Canada live in poverty. Another scholar states that "racialized group members are twice as likely as other Canadians to live in poverty" (Galabuzi, 2008, p. 87). New immigrants to Canada also suffer systemic or institutional discrimination as manifested in the difficulty of getting foreign credentials recognized and discrimination in hiring practices (Wallis & Kwok, 2008); this occurs despite Canada's economic dependence on immigrants. Ethnic minorities and Aboriginal people continue to experience poorer health, increased contact with the criminal justice system, exposure to violence, and poverty (Galabuzi, 2008): all risk factors for homelessness.

A substantial body of research has attempted to identify risk factors that have led to people becoming homeless (Fitzpatrick, Kemp, & Klinker, 2000):

- childhood maltreatment or trauma (one-time or continual).
- family conflict.
- being under the care of child welfare.
- a history of criminal activity and prison stays.

- service in the armed forces.
- absence of social supports.
- accumulated debt.
- addictions with drugs and alcohol.
- limited educational background and job-related skills.
- mental health issues.
- poor physical health and/or disability.

Additional factors have been identified which include being a woman, a recent immigrant, an ethnic minority, or an Aboriginal person (Galabuzi, 2008), and having been raised in a poor family (Ismael, 2006).

In many cases, these risk factors for homelessness occur together and serve to exacerbate the risk of homelessness. For example, an adult who was abused as a child is at higher risk of developing a mental illness or a substance addiction and has fewer positive social supports (Herman, 1992), thus increasing the susceptibility to homelessness. The immediate impetus for homelessness may be the result of crisis situations that cannot be immediately resolved. Research summarized by Fitzpatrick, Kemp, and Klinker (2000) identifies some of these triggers:

- children leaving home as a result of a parental conflict.
- divorce, separation, or death of a partner.
- being released from service in the armed forces.
- leaving a care facility or a prison.
- increase in substance abuse.
- impending financial burden.
- mental health breakdown.
- loss of home (whether rented or owned).
- relocating to a new city for work and finding no available housing.

Research has identified preventative interventions that decrease an individual's risk of homelessness:

- providing housing advice and services of aid.
- creating services that reduce social isolation and improving accessibility to these services.
- providing rental supports for people with mental health issues or addictions problems.
- giving supports to people who are about to lose their home for reasons of divorce, widowhood, or isolation.

- increasing school-based educational programs on homelessness and 'running away'.
- increasing outreach services.
- providing mediation between parents and youth.
- aiding people to return to their home area if needed.
- providing tenancy support for adults of all ages.
- extending support for youth transitioning from foster care.
- developing programs that aid those from the armed forces and prisons to secure housing. (Fitzpatrick, Kemp, & Klinker, 2000; Lindholm, 1991; Randall & Brown, 1999; Yanetta & Third, 1999).

Homeless shelters, like other forms of social housing, need to be understood within the broader perspective of Canadian social policy (Graham, Swift, & Delaney, 2008). Poverty, or insufficient income, is frequently a causal factor for homelessness, and the prevalence of poverty in a city, province, or country has broad structural causes. For example, in Alberta, some scholars believe that the provincial government has not undertaken the necessary means to prevent poverty and, thus, reduce homelessness in this province (Graham & Kuiken, 2007). Some reasonable interventions could be the implementation of a *living wage* – the minimum hourly wage necessary for a person to achieve some specific standard of living – rather than a minimum wage, and the implementation of income support programs that could actually provide sufficient income to pay market-based rents (Graham & Kuiken, 2007). Inadequate income support programs at the provincial level (Assured Income for the Severely Handicapped [AISH]) or at the federal level (Canadian Child Tax Benefit [CCTB]) are part of the broader context in which homelessness occurs and is perpetuated (Graham, 2007).

A number of homelessness prevention strategies focus on adjusting and expanding the role of social service agencies that homeless people typically contact (Raising the Roof, 2001). Homeless shelters themselves may be important places for a variety of individual homelessness prevention services, such as outreach services helping people to get off and stay off the streets. But these services are ineffective if there are insufficient housing resources. There are various alternative models of intervention to consider, including a Housing First approach – that seeks to provide housing to at risk people and then address other psychosocial issues such as addiction, mental health, employment, or education. This kind of approach has proven extremely successful in Portland, Oregon, where permanent housing has been created for approximately 1,500 of the city's 4,000 homeless individuals within the first year of implementation (Canadian Broadcasting Corporation, 2008).

Decreasing an individual's risk of homelessness will not eliminate homelessness altogether: reducing homelessness within any population also requires changes and interventions directed at the levels of governments and other institutions. NIMBY, or "not in my back yard", describes the response from communities when its members "perceive a local development as a threat to their land values, way of life, or health and safety" (Shier, Walsh, & Graham, 2007, p. 67). For any strategy to improve the lives of the homeless successfully, public perceptions regarding poverty and homelessness must be made less negative. Educating and demystifying issues surrounding the region's homelessness and the location of homeless shelters could provide an initial focus for this change.

Local business groups and organizations can, and have, collaborated in creating a more productive perspective of homelessness for the whole community (Walsh, Graham, & Shier, in press). In Portland, the city's police department has contributed funds to the city's housing initiative from their own budget; as they are commonly the first point of contact for homeless individuals, they recognized that housing homeless individuals will ultimately save their department – and taxpayers – money (CBC, 2008). Meanwhile, a 2007 Sheldon Chumir Foundation study estimates the financial cost of homelessness in Canada to be between $4.5 and $6 billion annually in expenditures within the criminal justice, health and social service sectors, as well as in emergency shelter costs (Laird, 2007). Whether contributing funds is possible or not, it is often useful for shelters to work in a continuing, close partnership with local police departments and community members to ensure that both the general public and shelter clients feel safe in the area around the shelter and feel involved in decisions made by shelter management.

In the city of Victoria, British Columbia, as in other cities, police officers team up with mental health practitioners and patrol together in order to better serve the safety needs of the homeless population and the larger community (CBC, 2008). Collaboration could also occur through the implementation of a "good neighbor" program in which everyone in the community from homeless shelter clientele to other residents of the community congregate to a common goal, such as agreeing on policies to increase safety such as shelter curfew, or policies to clean up the community such as picking up litter. Also, community members may be willing to volunteer, either at the shelter directly or on the board of directors. This would make community collaboration more continual than a one-time or annual event. Portland officials now concur that the key issue to ending homelessness in a sustainable manner is identifying affordable housing initiatives as being part of the community's infrastructure, similar to schools or parks (CBC, 2008). As we will elaborate in Chapter 2, the spatial characteristics of a homeless shelter can significantly determine a community's acceptance (or lack thereof) of a homeless shelter. For example, shelters that require clientele to line up on sidewalks outside the building can both compromise client dignity and invoke public criticism of the shelter's presence in the community.

Homeless Shelters

Homeless shelters are one response to the issue of homelessness; this form of intervention has developed over time for a variety of reasons and has become increasingly prevalent within the past century. As a permanent part of the urban environment, shelters must be integrated in ways that meet the needs of both homeless individuals and other community members. Those managing homeless shelters must simultaneously consider the interests of all stakeholders. The location of these shelters, the services that are offered, and the interactions that homeless people have with their communities are all influenced by perceptions held by the community.

Those at risk of being homeless or who are homeless already may live in specific communities to gain access to employment or housing opportunities (Wolch & Dear, 1993) or simply because they are trying to survive, meet basic needs, and have access to social services (Cloke, Widdowfield, & Milbourne, 2000). Shelters therefore may be built in neighborhoods that are already under-empowered (DeVereuil, 2006; Veness, 1994), poor (Dear & Wolch, 1987; Rowe & Wolch, 1990), or both. Homeless people often experience a reduction in mobility, so shelters are located in places that are within walking or transit range of other services – particularly health and social. As with many neighborhoods, people may remain within close geographic parameter to where they live and work; this is also the case with homeless people and, thus, they may be limited in interaction with other communities in any given city (Marcuse, 1988; Rowe & Wolch, 1990). A number of scholars describe the geographic location of homeless shelters as potentially restrictive for homeless people (Takahashi, 1998) and as exacerbating exclusionary processes that may already exist for these populations (Sibley, 1995). Here there may develop a polarization resulting in strong delineations between those who are similar to *us* and all others, *them*. People fear what they do not know and those whom they do not encounter. Homeless people are often isolated from the larger communities within which they reside; this may lead some outside that geographic community to develop negative views of homeless people (Kennedy & Fitzpatrick, 2001; Kennett, 1994; Pleace, 1998). Oftentimes this isolation is compounded by the isolation associated with various other personal characteristics, such as prior criminal history or having a mental illness. Homelessness and other forms of isolation perpetuate each other.

Scholars note that homeless people may be forced to meet their basic needs of survival under the guise of scrutiny (Hartnett & Harding, 2005). In Canadian cities, and in other parts of the world, myriad anti-homeless laws make public vagrancy illegal, and so police may arrest and detain people simply because they are homeless (Davis, 1990; Simon, 1996; Soja, 2000; Vergara, 1995). Such legislation is frequently motivated to restrict the homeless from being in *public spaces* and limit the areas and communities in which homeless people may physically be present; thus, there is a social control component to homeless shelters as well (Mitchell, 1997; Smith, 1996).

Neighborhood Mobility & Life Cycles

Both social and spatial elements of places move through periods of prosperity, decay, and rejuvenation. A community is a collection of spatial and social places which are defined by structures and boundaries. The perceptions that people hold affect communities: the ways in which communities and neighborhoods interact can impact members' ability to support socially inclusive or exclusive practices over time. According to Smith and Peters (1987), *neighborhood*, in sociological terms, consists of "the degree of social organization, the nature and quality of social interaction arising from propinquity and shared fate, and the relative vitality of the social networks found in urban neighborhoods" (p. 109). Neighborhood mobility, then, is a process by which spatial and social components change throughout time, and socially inclusive (or socially exclusive) practices become the by-product of this joint process of change.

Middle- and upper-class populations in cities have created suburban neighborhoods to escape from the stresses of the city or workplace and to deal with the inescapable conflicts of socioeconomic disparity in public society (Sennett, 1970a, 1970b). Here, we see the rise of homogeneous enclaves of social classes following neighborhood boundaries and the difficulties for large segments of society to respond positively to diversity within the city. Neighborhoods, which were once socially and economically diverse, increasingly have developed into zones of homogeneity, sometimes ethnically and economically based (Galabuzi, 2008). Gentrification is best understood as follows: "when affluent residents begin moving into non-affluent neighborhoods in large enough number to make a change in the overall composition of the area" (Kleniewski, 2002, p. 114). This process can have a very negative impact on low-income residents: people who can no longer afford to purchase homes at market prices or pay rents in inner city communities have no other option but to leave (Hartman, 1979). But it can also be a positive thing, revitalizing communities and entire neighborhoods and cities (Freeman & Braconi, 2004; Sumka, 1979). The ideal of physical boundaries in gated communities is particularly pervasive, emerging in cities across North America over the last two decades. Many new upscale housing developments are being walled off from the surrounding community (Kleniewski, 2002). By restricting movement and constructing physical boundaries, gated communities explicitly define both membership and non-membership. Such notions of belonging, however, are not restricted to physical barriers. Social interactions within a neighborhood influence similar inclusionary and exclusionary practices. In contrast either to gated communities or rampant gentrification: a vast literature focuses on the priority of a *social mix* to present positive interactions in socially inclusive neighborhoods (Rose, 2004). These concerns, as well as notions of goodness of fit, are salient to the next chapter on one homeless shelter in the city of Calgary.

Chapter 2

The Role Of Planning
and Urban Design

Much of our everyday urban existence occurs within the shared city spaces defined by both public and private buildings and made up of streets, sidewalks, parks, and squares. These elements, known collectively as the public realm, are spaces that all citizens can occupy by right. They primarily provide access to homes, offices, public buildings, and places of entertainment and culture. They also offer space for the many other functions traditionally associated with urban life, such as markets, public festivals, and, importantly, the ad hoc meetings and happenings that make urban life *urban*. The public realm is also the domain of the homeless. It is where they spend much of their time, and where some of them are forced to take care of human needs, such as rest, sleep, socializing, and, sometimes urinating and defecating.

The urban experience is partly formed by the character and shape of the public realm's built edges, made up of both public and private components, and it influences the interactions that we have within its spaces. Private buildings usually form the edges and act to define and articulate public space. The public components (sidewalks, streets, and public open spaces) are part of the same composition. The street is a major component of the public realm. This chapter illustrates the relationship between the public realm and shelter services and identifies ways in which these social service organizations can relate to their surrounding public space.

Evolution of Urban Form and Quality – The Calgary Example

The form of an object or organism (including the form of the city as a whole or of the public realm components) is a "diagram of the forces" that have acted upon it (Thompson, 1961, p. 11), and in urban form, these forces include physical as well as cultural forces. The evolution of the public realm reflects the evolution of ideas and ideologies. The values placed on the built landscape by cultures are reflected in changing patterns of land ownership and land development and, consequently, are also reflected in the spatial qualities of the public realm. Reviews of the evolution of North American twentieth-century physical planning and design, and the physical forms produced as expressions of the values held at the time, provide great insight into contemporary perspective (Relph, 1987; Sandalack & Nicolai, 1998; Sandalack & Nicolai, 2006; Vidler 1996).

The first phase of urban development in most of the western world continued until approximately 1940. It was marked by incremental changes to older forms as new technologies and concepts were introduced. Architects and urbanists considered the problems of town planning and design in terms of historical precedent, context, and propriety. The public realm was an important part of civic infrastructure, and many of the significant public spaces and streets of contemporary cities were established during this period. Street form and pattern usually extended and grafted onto an existing framework.

Most cities and towns in North America are less than 200 years old – many barely a century – and have been rapidly transformed from primitive conditions to total modernity. Most of these cities were planned around a central public space, with a hierarchy of streets and public open spaces extending outward. For example, the original plan for Calgary featured a grid network of streets, typical of towns and cities built on the western railway. The first commissioned city plan was prepared by Thomas Mawson in 1914. Mawson envisioned a system of streets, civic spaces, and squares focused on the rivers, and modeled after the *City Beautiful* movement. The plan was clearly based on a strong vision of the public realm and its importance; owing to the combination of an economic downturn, the First World War, and the inappropriateness of some of Mawson's architectural ideas, it was never carried out.

The second phase corresponds to modernism, corporate development, and the invention and institutionalization of methods for town planning, which coincided with the period of economic growth following World War II. This phase reached its zenith in the 1960s and 1970s and still continues to some extent. The paradigm of history was replaced by one of space, where architecture and urbanism attempted to express functional and experiential space. History, tradition, and local and regional identity were thought to be antiprogress and old-fashioned – huge pieces of our cities, towns, and landscapes were destroyed to make way for progress. The lifestyles that go along with the spatial forms that were produced – the housing projects, suburbs, shopping centres and strip malls – are now taken for granted, while at the same time they contribute to several contemporary urban problems, including suburban sprawl, decline of the central business district, and a neglect of the traditional public realm – the street and the public square.

Over time, town form became discontinuous (there was little attempt to graft newer developments onto the existing), building typology became less place specific – the international style and later a context-immune and style-less generic form predominated – the public realm declined (it was generally not required that buildings shape outdoor space), and place identity became vague and confused.

Zoning was one of the planning tools of choice at this time, and it aimed for, and resulted in, a pattern of distinct and separate land uses. In addition to functionally separating incompatible land uses, the Central Business District became distinct from the suburbs, in terms of relative density and intensity. The 1958 City Zoning Bylaw was far from a benign tool, as it started to put into play the processes that would result in the destructive practices of urban renewal of the 1960s and 1970s. Urban renewal was one of the planning strategies of the age, and it managed to destroy huge pieces of the downtown. It was an approach taken by many cities to try to get rid of actual and perceived blight and to encourage revitalization. In Calgary, the period of urban renewal was responsible for the destruction of much of the early fabric, and it set in motion several processes that are still influencing urban quality and function. The 1966 Calgary Downtown Master Plan (City of Calgary Planning Advisory Committee) was a highly influential document of this period. It recognized the continuing central role of the downtown and set out strategies to improve its accessibility and simplify its structure. Its policy thrusts were to reinforce the linear east-west axis, to introduce a pedestrian mall and a north-south walkway, and to consolidate the office core. It proposed plans to address "blight" in the east end, and it accepted that the desire of every person to drive and store his/her automobile in the downtown must be accommodated. An emphasis, therefore, was high capacity roads and interchanges. The 1966 Plan was a product of the values of the time that emphasized modernity and newness along with functional efficiency; its implementation brought on much demolition and rebuilding. Since Calgary was such a young city, this redevelopment had a devastating effect on any sense of historic continuity and a detrimental effect on the quality of the public realm.

Transportation was the emphasis; and the plan's number one objective was to double the number of cars that could enter the downtown. Two concentric ring-roads were intended to increase the downtown's vehicle-handling capacity, and a network of one-way couplets would feed several parking structures. It was during this time that 11th and 12th Avenues in the area in which the Mustard Seed Ministry is located started in particular to deteriorate. The plan attempted to spatially segregate different land uses, and various historical accounts of this time talk about the "negative heterogeneous land uses" that had been allowed to develop and that needed to be addressed. This contrasts with today's approach of encouraging mixed uses as a quality necessary to vibrancy.

The plan identified "six comprehensive renewal areas" in the downtown area which were found to have varying degrees of "substandardness," defined in terms of overcrowded homes, inadequate schools, parks and playgrounds, inadequate water and sewer services, and questionable use of downtown land. The plan hastened the demise of several downtown neighborhoods over the next decades, and lost were many of the amenities and services required to support residential development, including grocery stores, corner stores, and small retail businesses. The scene was carefully set for redevelopment. Several major projects were constructed in the downtown, with scores of buildings razed to make way for massive commercial and institutional buildings. Most of these were massive structures with little regard for the creation of the public realm of streets and squares that could have helped to define a more urban and pedestrian friendly city. Combined with the one-way streets and the prohibition of on-street parking, the resulting pedestrian quality was very poor. The east part of the city was therefore made very vulnerable. Without a residential population to keep "eyes on the street," it became the place where crime, marginal uses, and homeless people became concentrated.

In 1981, Calgary was awarded the right to host the 1988 Winter Olympics. This led to numerous exemplary projects that helped to give Calgary a different self-image and an international profile. It also brought Calgarians back downtown again for the medal ceremonies at Olympic Plaza. However, the required redevelopment also expedited urban clearance in the east part of the downtown and the Beltline area (comprised of the neighborhoods of Connaught and Victoria Park directly south of downtown and so named because of a streetcar line that once ran as a belt around the area), and the removal of the Greyhound Bus Depot from its downtown location to west of 14th Street SW, which placed it out of the range of easy walking from downtown, the railway station, and the LRT stations, hence eliminating what had become a gathering place for the homeless and other marginalized people.

Redevelopment of the East Village in Calgary is still stalled almost fifty years after urban renewal processes decimated the area. To date, only one high-quality condominium development has been constructed, and, with the extensive surface parking lots, the area is a disappointing underutilization of this prime downtown location. New social service facilities, including the Riverside Drop In and Rehab Centre and the Salvation Army Drop In Centre have been constructed. These facilities serve an important social service function and are of relatively high architectural quality, but in the absence of other balancing residential and commercial development, perceptions of this area as a backwater for criminal and marginal activities have been further entrenched.

Victoria Park has experienced continued deterioration over past decades, including the loss of the Co-op grocery store on 12th Avenue SE, one of the last inner city grocery stores, an incident that was both a cause and an indicator of a declining residential population. Currently the area is dominated by empty lots and surface parking, along with isolated office and residential uses and significant foot traffic generated around 11th Avenue Mustard Seed Ministry buildings. However, several new projects are underway, including plans for a high-end grocery market. The area has been renamed Victoria Crossing by the business community in order to promote its commercial potential as a mixed-use tourism/entertainment destination, a strategy that relies on imagery other than the area's primarily residential and warehouse heritage (Hiller & Moylan, 1999). There is growing indication of an urban renaissance in the area, and several high-quality office and residential developments have recently been constructed, signs that the area will undergo significant transformation, if the current economic conditions can be maintained long enough to complete all of the projects.

The Qualities of Good Urban Form

Critics of the placelessness of much of our contemporary urban form have effectively drawn attention to the general qualitative decline of public space in North America. Jane Jacobs was perhaps the most important author to bring the discussion of urban form into the mainstream with her book *The Death and Life of Great American Cities* (1961). Jacobs defended neighborhood form, especially the street, as the premiere public space, and emphasized the importance of achieving a certain density and intensity of urban form as a necessary prerequisite to vibrant urban life.

A number of theories of spatial structure have been formulated, with various ways of conceptualizing space. Kevin Lynch (1960) saw the city image as a system composed of five basic elements: paths, edges, districts, nodes, and landmarks (or monuments). These urban elements provide physical and psychological orientation; together they provide the significant features of the mental map that inhabitants form of their city. This organizing structure provides a framework by which neighborhood urban form, and its parts and the ways they are related, can be analyzed and then used as a basis for design. Lynch focused some of his criticism on the unsatisfying products of modern development and the lack of proper public urban spaces. Roger Trancik (1986) brought the term *lost space* into planning and design vocabulary – a new category made necessary by the proliferation of surface parking, empty lots, and traffic interchanges.

Manuel Iniquez, as quoted in Ellin's *Postmodern Urbanizm* (1996), summarized the concern about the loss of the public realm:

> The city, ancient or modern has some characteristics that define it forever: the street, the square, the public buildings, the residences have established between them, through a slow and uninterrupted process, laws of composition. If such compositional laws are forgotten, as in recent years, the City, deprived of measurement and proportion, corrupts the architectural components within it, creating a monstrous medley which can never be called a true City. (p. 25)

The quality of the public realm has an impact on all aspects of life, including perception of safety, ease of walking, and general comfort. How an area is designed also influences whether there are shops, schools, services, and recreation areas; it also influences how access to public transportation is made available by the city and used by its inhabitants. It is essential that the places we create and improve embody the principles of good urban design.

Various authors have identified qualities that are believed to be embodied by good cities and towns. Punter (1990) attempted to compare ideas from a number of authors as to what might constitute "fundamental principles for contemporary architecture and urban design" (p. 10). This review provides a useful framework, especially as it attempts to demonstrate the commonalities among the authors. While a list of what are believed to be universal qualities is a useful way of organizing principles from a vast field of research, in order to be more meaningful, and more place-specific, it must be filtered through a particular approach. Frampton acknowledged that "there really is no such thing as an authentic local or national culture due to centuries of cultural contact and underutilization" (cited in Ellin, 1996, p. 68). However, it is important to mediate the impact of globalization with elements peculiar to each place. In order to do so, it is useful to determine what contributes to regional identity and how to develop it. A combination of universal qualities of good places and the qualities particular to a region or place could be valuable in providing guidance for development of good places that are distinct.

A list of qualities important in Calgary downtown was developed by synthesizing several relevant authors (Bentley, Alcock, McGlynn, Murrain, & Smith, 1985; Hough, 1990; Jacobs, 1961; Lynch 1960, 1976, 1981; Paterson et al, 1994):

1. Legibility, order, and function (spatiality)
a) Places should possess visual order.
   – edges should be distinct; it should be evident when one is inside/outside a place.
b) Places should possess appropriate spatial order.
   – the public realm should consist of a series of linked public spaces.
c) Places should be permeable, with easy circulation for people and cars.
   – pedestrian circulation at the local level should be accommodated.
   – vehicle circulation should be accommodated.

2. Authentic identity (continuity)
a) Places should be expressive of their environmental context.
   – appropriate forms, materials, and spatial structure for climate should be apparent.
   – environmental process and form should be evident or be interpreted.
b) Places should be expressive of their local and regional history and responsive to change.
   – historical markers should be present; new markers should be encouraged.

3. Fitness
a) Places should possess biological fitness.
 – comfort and livability for residents should be design objectives.
 – microclimate should be modified to improve comfort.
b) Places should possess psychological and social fitness.
 – urban form should provide a feeling of shelter.
 – urban form should support and sustain a diverse urban population.
c) Places should be environmentally and economically sustainable.
 – an optimum balance between population and resources should be attained.

4. Process
a) Places should support the local community (commercial, retail, office, residential, and services sectors).
b) Individual rights and freedoms should be recognized and protected.
c) Environmental learning should be possible, where citizens can gain direct experience.
d) Places should evolve by slow, small, incremental changes.

The desirable qualities of the urban form should be particularly applied to the public realm. Public space is largely shaped by the buildings around its edges. When buildings are designed with attention only to the building envelope and the interior, then the space outside the building – the public realm – usually becomes lost space. However, when a more comprehensive approach is taken, it is more likely that the qualities of good urban form will be incorporated. Emphasis should be on quality of urban form and urban life, and the interrelationship of scales of thinking, rather than on traditional disciplinary concerns of buildings or land-use designations.

Good streets in Calgary and in cities worldwide share several features. Narrow lot subdivision, as an example, ensures that there are a variety of businesses, rather than just one large box, and enables shops to open onto the street, creating ample opportunities for people and products to go in and out. This is the quality of permeability that gives a higher degree of choice for the pedestrian and leads to a livelier and more interesting street. An active and continuous street of common building edges fronting onto an amply-proportioned and detailed sidewalk provides the setting for a pedestrian culture – and people always attract more people. Street trees, well-placed benches in sunny spots protected from the wind, and reduced clutter do wonders for creating a comfortable human scale (that is, design that is scaled to the dimensions of the human body, allowing people to relate more directly to their environment).

Urban Design as a Methodology for City Making

Downtown commercial and cultural activity has generally suffered as a consequence of the imposition of modernist planning and suburban development. Calgary's downtown, as one example, is presently composed of discrete functional zones as a result of previous development processes and planning initiatives. A more integrated city should be emphasized in which neighborhoods are linked, access is easier, and fewer empty lots interrupt the urban fabric. This will require undoing some of the damage that was caused by the urban renewal initiatives and by the imposition of functional zoning and the Plus 15 system (Calgary's above-ground indoor pedestrian network).

The land and landscape character is the most permanent aspect of the built environment, with the greatest potential to contribute to a sense of place. In much of the city, street trees and other plantings provide the best opportunity to reinforce landscape character. The public realm – that is, the shared city space made up of the streets, sidewalks, parks, squares and plazas – constitutes the next most permanent component of the built landscape. Several generations of built form will come and go within the life cycle of the urban structure, however if the infrastructure of the public realm is intact, then the built form has a sense of continuity and meaning over time. Each building, if it has a resiliency of form, may be used for various activities or programs. This robustness of built form contributes further to the establishment of a sense of place through continuity of form.

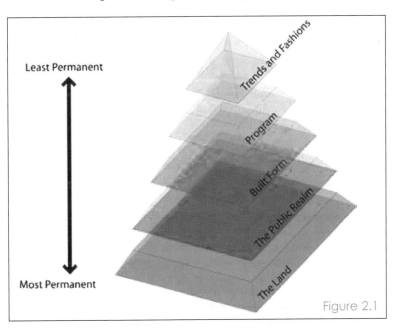

Least Permanent

Most Permanent

Trends and Fashions

Program

Built Form

The Public Realm

The Land

Figure 2.1

The least permanent aspects of the built environment, and of design activity, are the transient and ephemeral trends and fashions. While these frequently add the qualities of delight and contemporariness to the built environment, there is normally a built-in obsolescence to them, and they should be understood as the least permanent, although not necessarily the least important, aspects of environmental design.

The Public Realm as Responsibility

It is the public realm, the spaces now created mostly by default, that needs to re-emerge as an important focus of the design and planning professions. The public realm consists of physical as well as metaphysical spaces. They have actual and symbolic value. The built environment can either diminish or increase our sense of place, and of our sense of being in the world (Kingwell, 2000). In order for urban designers to properly respond to criticisms of our changing contemporary urban form, education and practice need to be relevant. To do so, designers need to consider the public realm within a bigger picture of overall city form, process, and structure. Currently, as a society we devote more of our design attention to individual buildings, to programming, and especially to trends and fashions than to the most permanent elements: the public realm and the landscape. The less permanent elements come and go, but the public infrastructure persists and can give a sense of continuity and quality to a place. What has been neglected is design at the city scale and a focus on the public realm.

Physical Realm and Social Service Delivery

One of the most important roles of the city form is to offer hospitality to all of its residents. This goes beyond the basic provision of shelter; the form and arrangement of the city elements should allow residents to feel safe, comfortable, and part of a larger society. This is one aspect of sustainability – that all segments of society, from the rich to the poor and homeless, are considered important. Urban planning and design should accommodate all citizens, and should be especially sensitive to the needs of the less fortunate, who are often not in a position to be able to effect change. The urban form is, and should be, more than a collection of streets and buildings: it is also an arrangement of places to which people may develop significant relationships. Many cities within North America have not been successful at including people experiencing homelessness in the wider social context of the city, further marginalizing their roles within their local neighborhoods and communities. To address this concern, in relation to the physical aspects of shelter organizations, a five stage research design was conceptualized and carried out by the authors – a joint effort between Environmental Design and Social Work scholars (see Figure 2.2). The rationale and findings from each of the research design stages are described in detail within each of the sections. The remainder of this chapter describes the design considerations taken into account by the Environmental Design team; Chapter Three provides details of a precedent analysis carried out by the Social Work research team, with the concluding chapter illustrating the recommendations based on the combined efforts of data collection.

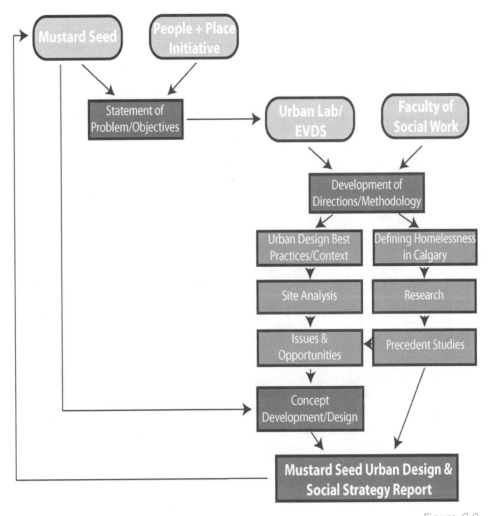

Figure 2.2

Physical Analysis of the Mustard Seed Street Ministry

The Mustard Seed Street Ministry is a faith-based organization established in 1972 to address the growing issue of homelessness in Calgary. It has undergone much expansion and evolution and today faces the pressures of the city's rapidly growing homeless population. Mustard Seed programming is distributed among three buildings. The oldest building, Centre 102, provides basic services, including food and emergency beds on the main floor, access to donor-supplied clothing banks on the second, and transitional housing on the third and fourth. It moved to its current location in Centre 102 in 1992 in response to increasing demand for its services, and it has continued to refine its scope as a non-profit organization in Calgary. The Mustard Seed has further expanded its facilities in recent years, incorporating The Creative Centre across the street from Centre 102, and this year acquired the land immediately north of Centre 102 with plans of developing high-density affordable housing.

The Creative Centre offers support for the Mustard Seed's mid- to long-term guests, progressive educational and employment programming,

Image 2.1: Centre 102 with a donation truck in front.

classrooms, computer labs, and counseling staff. Recreational and artistic activities are often organized through the Creative Centre, and health programs are offered for guests in step-up and transitional housing. These two buildings are under intense pressure to expand their capacity.

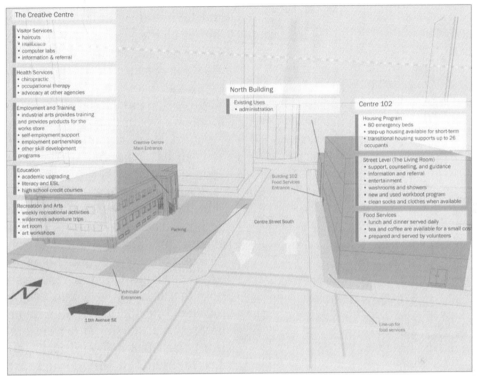

Image 2.2

The recently-acquired building north of Centre 102 will allow some programming shifts within the agency, and the emergency shelter services will likely be relocated to the main floor. This could free up room for food services in Centre 102. The Seed's administrative functions, which have been housed on part of the top floor of the north building for over a year, will be able to expand in this space along with the Creative Centre expansion.

One option currently being considered by the Mustard Seed Ministry is construction of a twenty-eight-storey building on the site of the north building. The intent is to provide a mix of transitional, subsidized, and affordable housing, along with other services.

The Mustard Seed faces increasing pressure in the developing Beltline community. High-end condominium towers and block redevelopments, fueled by the city's economic prosperity, are rapidly changing the charac-

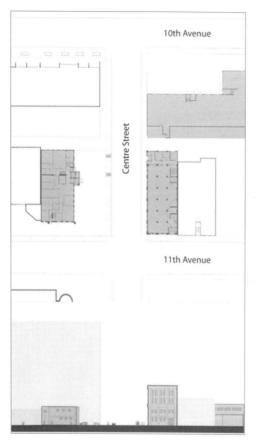

10th Avenue

Centre Street

11th Avenue

Image 2.3

ter and composition of the neighborhood. The need for affordable housing in Calgary has come into conflict with increasing land values, major population increases, and high-end development, creating a challenging political and economic environment for the Mustard Seed. As it moves to expand the scale and scope of its services in the city's core, it is increasingly important that the Mustard Seed respond appropriately to its social and spatial contexts.

In order to gain a better understanding of the Mustard Seed site and the context within which it exists, an analysis of several factors was carried out. Some of the analysis provided insights into how the area evolved, and others provide information that will be helpful in proposing interventions into the urban condition and development of higher quality public spaces.

Historic Evolution of Beltline Area

The evolution of several blocks within the Beltline area surrounding the Mustard Seed illustrates how the fabric of fine-grained, single family housing of the early 1900s was eventually replaced by a coarser-grained pattern that included numerous gaps and surface parking lots. Although many of these gaps have recently or are currently been filled by new developments, the result is a discontinuous urban fabric without a strong resident population. Homeless and other marginalized people eventually sought refuge in these areas and the neighborhood developed a negative reputation.

Image 2.4

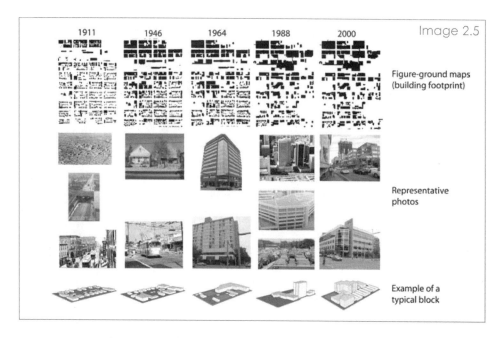

Image 2.5

Figure-ground maps
(building footprint)

Representative
photos

Example of a
typical block

Distribution of Social Services

The Mustard Seed site is one of several social services found in Calgary's downtown. Many of these are concentrated in the eastern part of the area, partly as a result of the urban deterioration that occurred over the past several decades. This concentration also contributes to the negative stigma attached to the east part of Calgary.

Image 2.6

Environmental Conditions

Studies of sun and wind around Mustard Seed indicate where shelter from the elements is required and reveal locations that may be opportunities for public space development.

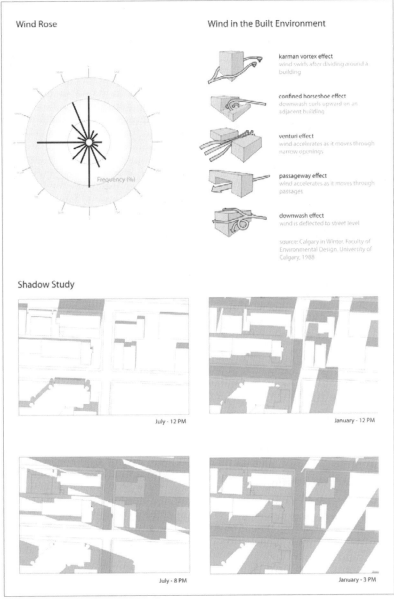

Image 2.7

Existing Utilities and Infrastructure

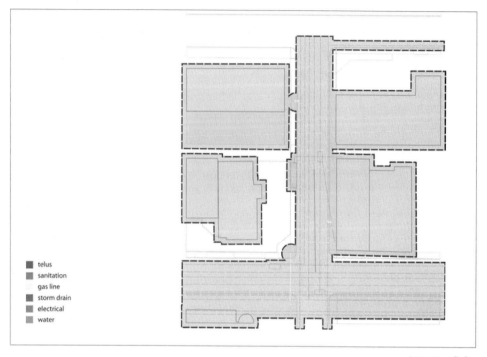

telus
sanitation
gas line
storm drain
electrical
water

Image 2.8

Existing Land Use

Land uses in the area have changed from almost exclusively residential in the early part of the 1900s to a coarse-grained mix of office, some retail, parking, and empty lots. This situation is currently in rapid transition, as numerous high-density highrise condominium projects, many with a mixed-use component at their base, are under construction or in the planning phase. The Mustard Seed site finds itself in a redeveloping context in which its activities will be in a much higher profile; any redevelopment needs to consider this current urban transition.

Vehicle & Transit Circulation

Circulation and parking in the area around the Mustard Seed currently favors the automobile. There are numerous surface parking lots, contributing to a poor quality pedestrian environment, and the one-way couplet of 11th and 12th Avenues carry large volumes of car traffic. The railway tracks just to the north of the Mustard Seed site form a strong barrier to easy pedestrian circulation between the downtown and the Beltline, and the existing railway underpasses are of a poor visual and experiential quality. Pedestrian circulation is therefore not well supported.

Patterns of Use in the Public Realm

Through direct observation and informal interviews conducted with guests, volunteers, and Mustard Seed (MS) staff, patterns of human activity (including patterns of the homeless) were mapped. There is a strong corridor of gathering spaces that extends from from Memorial Park (MP) to the southwest of the Mustard Seed to Olympic Plaza (OP) to the northeast. Public parks and empty lots are more frequently used by the homeless, while open spaces adjacent to office buildings are utilized by office workers. There is also a strong corridor connecting many of the social service agencies that is used by those persons utilizing the services or seeking shelter.

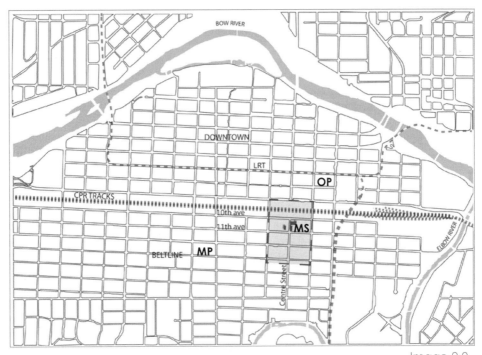

Image 2.9

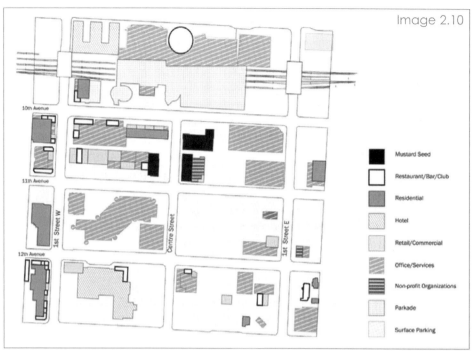

Image 2.10

- Mustard Seed
- Restaurant/Bar/Club
- Residential
- Hotel
- Retail/Commercial
- Office/Services
- Non-profit Organizations
- Parkade
- Surface Parking

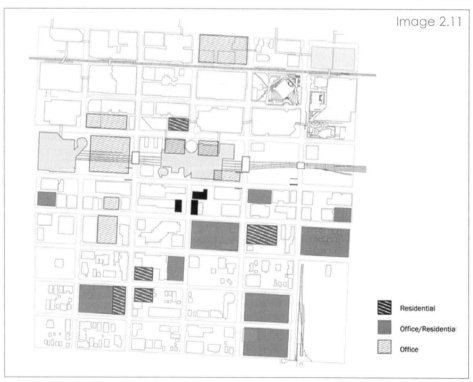

Image 2.11

- Residential
- Office/Residentia
- Office

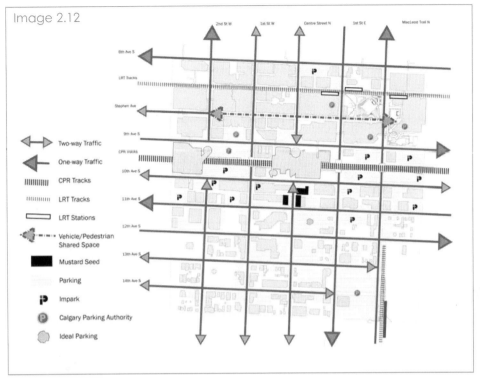

Image 2.12

2nd St W 1st St W Centre Street N 1st St E MacLeod Trail N

6th Ave S
LRT Tracks
Stephen Ave
9th Ave S
CPR Tracks
10th Ave S
11th Ave S
12th Ave S
13th Ave S
14th Ave S

Two-way Traffic
One-way Traffic
CPR Tracks
LRT Tracks
LRT Stations
Vehicle/Pedestrian Shared Space
Mustard Seed
Parking
Impark
Calgary Parking Authority
Ideal Parking

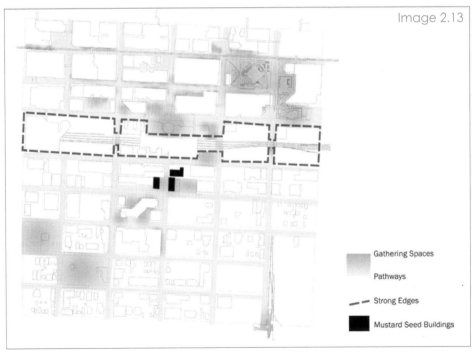

Image 2.13

Gathering Spaces
Pathways
Strong Edges
Mustard Seed Buildings

Key Issues from the Site Analysis

A number of key issues arose out of the analysis and through discussions with Mustard Seed staff, and through interviews with business owners in the area:

1. Mustard Seed guests currently line up for meals and shelter along an open sidewalk with no protection from the elements.
2. Foot traffic between the two Mustard Seed buildings frequently takes place in midblock and is dangerous due to vehicular traffic.
3. Centre Street is lacking quality public space and streetscape in the rapidly evolving Beltline neighborhood.
4. There is a shortage and inaccessibility of public washrooms for the homeless.
5. Progressive programming and increased shelter demands require additional space for the Mustard Seed Ministry.
6. Safety and security are perceived to be of concern.

It is interesting to note that the main issue identified by business owners was related to a perception of low safety. Although this is not substantiated through other data (i.e. there is no evidence of higher then normal rates of personal assaults, robberies or other crimes in this area compared with other parts of the downtown), the fact that many people perceive safety and security to be a concern presents another challenge to the redevelopment of the site.

Given the aspirations that the Mustard Seed Ministry has to expand its services and improve its public spaces, and the rapidly evolving urban context within which the Mustard Seed is situated, there is an excellent opportunity to consider how this homeless shelter and social services provider might be redeveloped so that it accomplishes its goals, while contributing positively to Calgary's urban environment. In order to better understand the opportunities and constraints of this general issue (i.e. integrating a social service facility into a contemporary city) numerous sites throughout North America and elsewhere were studied; Chapter Three presents several of these available precedents

---

Author's Note: Since the preparation of this manuscript, the Mustard Seed Ministry has altered its delivery of services and has relocated its emergency housing to a site in the industrial area near Macleod Trail and 50th Avenue SE. It has also received City Council approval for the development of its proposed highrise housing structure. However, since construction in Calgary has recently experienced some economic challenges, it is not certain when this project will be completed.

Chapter 3

Precedent Research

A globalizing capitalist economy has encouraged cities throughout the developed world to focus on the maintenance of a high level of capital and a large middle class population (Cox, 1997; Ley, 1996; Sandalack & Nicolai, 2006). In order for cities to remain competitive in this kind of economy, and for cities to be livable, safe, interesting, and pleasant places, a particular level of attractiveness is necessary (Murphy, 2000). City planners, administrators, and other stakeholders in developed countries have come to value sound urban planning and design as involving a mix of uses and a mix of demographics in creating good urban form and an equitable and civil city (building on the qualities of urban form as outlined in Bentley, Alcock, McGlynn, Murrain, and Smith (1985); Lynch (1981); Trancik (1986); and others. Minimal research to date, though, considers the fit of social service delivery systems within prevailing models of urban development.

The authors carried out site visits at sixty-three shelters throughout Canada, the United States, and the United Kingdom. Our research also took us to select sites in South America, Central America, and Africa. In all, we took photographs of spatial conditions in which shelter for homeless people are situated. At the North American and European sites, we also conducted interviews with shelter operators in which we gathered information about shelter services, spatial characteristics, and community perspectives of the shelter. From this analysis, we present potentially helpful methods for the design and spatial construction of homeless shelters. Our data particularly touches on ways of decreasing social experiences as isolation, segregation, and stigmatization.

Identifying Successful Shelter Precedents

The shelters showcased in this chapter were identified through a mixed-method process of qualitative interviews with fifty expert, key-informant practitioners in the area of homelessness and urban planning in North America and Europe, and through an extensive audit of secondary and primary literature sources. Analysis of both sources, the key-informant interviews, and the literature audit helped us to conceptualize successful shelter service delivery based on the interplay between factors associated with the built environment, community relationships, and the systemic characteristics of the shelter (Shier, Walsh, & Graham, 2007). The first theme, the built environment, includes shelter congruency, shelter size, shelter location and accessibility, and a shelter's community impact. The second theme, community relationships, includes perceptions of the homeless and of public safety, the challenges of NIMBYism, and positive community involvement. Finally, the third theme, systemic characteristics of a shelter, includes such characteristics as shelter programs, shelter management, and shelter attention to client dignity and safety (Shier, Walsh, & Graham, 2007). Successful shelter designs implemented the mutually reinforcing factors of client-focused, dignified service; many also had a positive way of integrating and cohering with the urban environment.

Following the key-informant stage of research, shelter directors were contacted and researchers conducted qualitative interviews with program administration personnel to confirm and expand upon findings from the literature and key-informant interviews. These interviews helped further conceptualize factors associated with the built environment, community relationships, and service delivery that create successful shelter situations for people experiencing homelessness (Walsh, Graham, & Shier, in press). Findings showed that success in service delivery was largely defined by an overlap of several characteristics associated with the three major themes identified above – systemic characteristics of a shelter, community relationships, and the built environment. In particular, many shelters can adequately foster client-centred and dignified services to guests of shelters. But, as has been discussed throughout this book, successful services extend beyond the immediate programming level within shelters and needs to consider the implications of the built environment and the surrounding community.

All shelter operators talked about the difficulty of serving clients within the demands of the physical structure, and compromises that are made in this regard, such as having fewer beds/rooms in favor of having more space/privacy for guests. These compromises also influenced service provision, as well as the location and size of administrative areas. Many shelter operators/administrators were also concerned about protecting clients from the public – specifically from predators or other potential harms. For example, a shelter visited in Soho, London had a curfew so that youth would not be exposed to various activities in the London nightlife. Another example, the Astoria shelter in New York provides services to transgendered youth. Its clients were at risk within the surrounding community, and its administrators highlighted concerns regarding the impact of lighting and entryways on client privacy and protection.

As for location, most shelter managers talked about the need to be accessible to the populations served but also feared the risk to many clients who moved to the inner city. The need for easy access to other health, social services, and educational services were often factors determining location, particularly if children or youth were the clientele. Clients of shelters are an exceptionally vulnerable group in society: this vulnerability can often be a combination of factors which increases their risk for homelessness to begin with, such as having a mental illness or having experienced abuse in childhood. Programming in the shelter itself or other agencies as well as positive community relationships may reduce these vulnerabilities.

Not all shelters analyzed in this research would be considered successful in all respects. The Salvation Army (Image 3.1) in Whitehorse, Yukon Territory prides itself on its service delivery, attention to client dignity, positive community relationships (such as managing NIMBY challenges). It maintains positive involvement with the surrounding community and alters programming to suit local needs. However, it is less successful regarding themes associated with the built environment: the shelter's physical and spatial congruency with the surrounding community and the shelter's physical impact in the community in which it is located (Figure 3.1). An example of a shelter that qualifies as successful across all considerations is the Wiseman Centre (Image 3.2) in St. John's, Newfoundland – a transitional housing model that offers single rooms to upwards of twenty homeless men.

Historically, when processes of urban renewal are undertaken, the social and economic implications to vulnerable people are often not considered. Instead, focus has been on the creation of new physical structures and architectural forms (McLeod, 2002; Sandalack & Nicolai 1998). As explored in Chapter Two, competing interests with different levels of power in urban planning often make the process of urban renewal complex, and municipal social policy may not be well connected to economic, spatial, or knowledge mobilization policy. It may also be haphazard, highly subject to competing interests (van den Berg, van der Meer, & Pol, 2003), and not always responsive to society's most vulnerable (Wacquant, 1999). A case in point is "the repressive [and aggressive] policing of [the] homeless...a strategy of elites to maintain control of core commercial spaces" (Vitale, 2008, p. 26).

In Global South settings, the urban response to homelessness is often shantytowns – settlements, sometimes illegal, of impoverished people who live in dwellings constructed from scraps of wood, metal, and/or plastic. Usually located on the periphery of major cities, shantytowns invariably do not have proper sanitation, electricity, or telephone services. They may be highly populous, with numbers approaching or exceeding that of the neighboring city itself. Images taken of shanty-type developments in Lima, Peru (Image 3.3) and Ethiopia (Image 3.4), highlight another common theme also reflected in the photos that follow from North America and Europe: the segregation of homeless individuals both socially and spatially (von Mahs, 2005).

In North America and Europe, there is a widespread process of gentrification: the development of upscale residential neighborhoods in the place of previously deteriorating neighborhoods within the city core. There are economic and social factors at play, as cities seek to attract a workforce that has money, marketable skills, and is not socially excluded. A further social reality is gentrification's geographic displacement of people of lower socio-economic status from areas in which they can no longer afford to live (Hiller & Moylan 1999; Murphy, 2000), often resulting in social polarization within and between communities (van den Berg, van der Meer, & Pol, 2003). Shelter locations are sometimes primarily determined based on processes of gentrification and the desire to socially exclude homeless individuals from areas within the city of rejuvenated wealth and prosperity. Image 3.5 of Rolling Shelter in London, England (a shelter providing service to upwards of thirty-two adults in single and double room occupancy units) and Image 3.6 taken of Seaton House in Toronto, Ontario (a large dormitory shelter providing services to 100+ guests) exemplify this problem.

Image 3.1: Salvation Army, Whitehorse, Yukon Territory

Image 3.2: Wiseman Centre, St. John's, Newfoundland

This historical process of gentrification also acts as an important example of how changes to physical structures can lead to a new social reconstruction of community (Keiller, 1998). It also highlights how people's perceptions of their urban environment are subjective and therefore malleable (Jacobs, 2002). The physical location of a gentrified community does not change; but the changes brought about by gentrification can significantly alter peoples' attitudes and impressions of a particular spatial area (Mohan, 2002). Some cities have successfully implemented models of gentrification in which shelters have been included in the renewal process. This has occurred both in cases where

Image 3.5: Rolling Shelter, London

the shelter has been a long-term feature within the community and in the recent introduction of a shelter to a community during or after a process of urban renewal. The success of these shelters has been facilitated by a number of things, including positive social and psychological impacts that the built environment can have on person and place perception.

Image 3.6: Seaton House, Toronto

Shelter Characteristics

The sites of data collection included sixteen cities in Canada (Brantford, Cambridge, Hamilton, North York, Ottawa, and Toronto, Ontario; Montreal, Quebec; Fredericton, Moncton, and Saint John, New Brunswick; Halifax, Nova Scotia; Regina and Saskatoon, Saskatchewan; St. John's, Newfoundland; Vancouver, British Columbia; Whitehorse, Yukon Territory), seven cities in the United States (Atlanta, Georgia; Austin, Texas; Buffalo and New York, New York; and Oceanside, San Francisco, and San Diego, California), and two cities in England (London and Manchester). Table 1 identified the entire sample of shelters or agencies that provide services to homeless individuals that were analyzed for this research.

Canada

Brantford	St. Leonard's Youth Resource Centre
Cambridge	The Bridges
Fredericton	Chrysalis
	Men's Shelter and Grace House
Halifax	Adsum House
	Metro Turning Point
	Phoenix Youth Shelter
Hamilton	Good Shepherd Centre
	Good Shepherd Family Centre
Moncton	Harvest House
Montreal	Le Chaînon
North York	Horizons for Youth
Ottawa	O'Connor House
	Carling Family Centre
Regina	Soul's Harbour Rescue Mission
	Waterston Centre
Saint John	Coverdale Shelter
	First Steps Housing Project
	Homeless Women's Shelter Services Inc.
Saskatoon	Choices for Youth
	Downtown Saskatoon Youth Centre
	Infinity House
St. John's	Naomi Centre
	Wiseman Centre
Toronto	Fred Victor Mission
	Massey Centre for Women
	Seaton House
	Woodgreen Family and Child Centre

Vancouver	Aboriginal Youth Safe House
	DEYAS
	Lookout Emergency Aid
	The Gathering Place
	The Vivian
	Powell Place
	Union Gospel Mission
Whitehorse	Kuashees Place
	Many Rivers Outreach
	Skookum Jim Friendship Centre
	Whitehorse Salvation Army

England

London	Berwick Street Centrepoint
	Endell Street Shelter
	Endsleigh Gardens
	Rolling Shelter
	Salvation Army Booth House Resettlement Centre
Manchester	Coops Foyer

United States

Atlanta	Atlanta Children's Shelter
	CHRIS Kids
Austin	Austin Resource Center for the Homeless
Buffalo	Buffalo City Mission
	Buffalo Downtown City Mission
	The Franciscan Center
New York	The Bowery Mission
	Carmen's Place
	The Christopher
	The Prince George
	The Times Square
Oceanside	House of Mary, Ann, Mary, and Ida
San Diego	Rachel's Night Shelter
	San Diego Rescue Mission
	Storefront Youth Shelter
San Francisco	Hospitality House
	Huckleberry House
	Larkin Street Youth Services Center

The characteristics of the shelters analyzed (i.e. shelter size, location, population served, and style) varied throughout these cities. These characteristics are described by the following four figures.

Figure 3.1 – Shelter size: Approximate number of people accessing shelter at one time

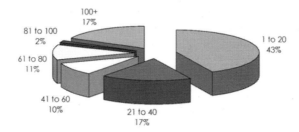

Figure 3.2 – Shelter location: Residential, service, and mixed communities

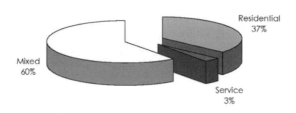

Figure 3.3 – Population served: Gender and age distinctions

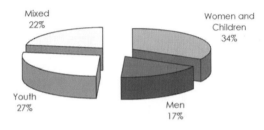

Mixed
22%

Women and
Children
34%

Youth
27%

Men
17%

Figure 3.4 – Shelter style: Model of shelter space afforded guests

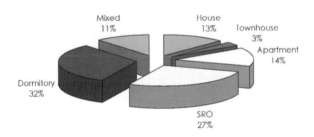

Mixed
11%

House
13%

Townhouse
3%

Apartment
14%

Dormitory
32%

SRO
27%

Each of these shelters and their support services for the homeless are distinct. The type of shelter afforded individuals, the size of the shelter, the population served, and the location of the shelter are a result of a number of factors, including identified local needs within each particular city. These factors illustrate an important point argued throughout this chapter and the next. Shelter service cannot be replicated exactly from one community to the next. Each needs to evolve within its uniquely local circumstances. This research has shown, though, that various factors can still be identified, and also generalized, to help improve the design and situation of shelters from one city to the next. The remainder of this chapter identifies those characteristics that are related to the built environment.

Characteristics of the Built Environment

Analysis of photographs of shelter precedents provided two conceptual categories to consider when developing or redeveloping shelters for the homeless: shelter spatiality and shelter integration. Shelter spatiality includes characteristics of the physical structure of the shelter within the context of the urban landscape. Shelter integration involves characteristics of the physical structure of the shelter in relation to the surrounding community in which the shelter is located. Both categories mutually reinforce the success of a particular shelter, and both have direct impact on the type of services offered and processes associated with service delivery.

Shelter Spatiality

Three conceptual themes may be considered in relation to the built environment: shelter location, shelter design, and shelter size. Each has a bearing on how and what shelter services are delivered, access to these services, and ways in which shelters and the communities in which they are situated both function. The shelter location draws attention to the zoned area of the shelter and includes factors related directly to the public realm – the presence of sidewalks, entrances and exits, and surrounding landscaping. The physical design of the shelter draws attention to exterior design mechanisms within the built environment, as well as the shelter's interior design. Our analysis pays particular attention to external physical design considerations; shelter interiors are worthy of further research but are beyond the scope of this book. A final consideration is the physical size of the shelter building.

Shelter Location

A key factor we considered is a shelter's physical location within a city. Traditionally, shelters have been built in urban neighborhoods that already housed individuals of a lower socio-economic status (Dear & Wolch, 1987; Rowe & Wolch, 1990). Shelters also tend to be located in places that are within walking or transit range of other social services, as people experiencing homelessness often experience a reduction in mobility. Interaction with other communities and services can be significantly reduced (Marcuse, 1988; Rowe & Wolch, 1990). DeVereuil (2006) and Veness (1994) argue that the development of large shelters in a socially excluded, lower-income neighborhood creates a "warehousing" strategy and contributes to the spatial control of homeless people. Thus the geographic location of homeless shelters can become considerably restrictive for homeless populations (Takahashi, 1998). The choices for shelter among individuals who are homeless are already severely limited, and the communities in which they live are, to a large extent, also chosen for them. By virtue of where they are located, as well as their design, social housing can contribute further to the social exclusion of the homeless (Sibley, 1995) and the perpetuation of their poverty and homelessness. Those who fear the homeless or perceive the homeless as deviant may want to see them isolated, segregated, or both (Kennedy & Fitzpatrick, 2001; Kennett, 1994; Pleace, 1998). To be sure, homeless people are often in public spaces. When they are in the public realm, some may feel that they are under the guise of scrutiny (Hartnett & Harding, 2005); many, too, may take on the publicly perceived role of what being homeless person represents. A sad old saying has it that the trouble with poverty is that it takes up all of one's time; likewise, many homeless find that the role of being homeless becomes the defining attribute of their existence in relation to public perception of their individualized situations (Anderson, 1998).

For these and other reasons, shelter location has a direct impact on dignified service delivery for people experiencing homelessness. The shelters photographed represent vastly different choices of location – some are located in residential communities and others in mixed residential and commercial communities. Image 3.7 of the Salvation Army Booth House Resettlement Centre in London, England, a shelter for upwards of 150 homeless men, illustrates a shelter in a mixed residential and commercial neighborhood. Image 3.8 of Horizons of Youth in Toronto a shelter for upwards of thirty-five homeless and/or at-risk youth, captures a shelter located in a solely residential neighborhood.

So much of urban planning depends on situation and context. Our analysis did not reveal evidence that there is an ideal zoning district that is the most appropriate for shelter services. Successful shelters were equally found within residential and mixed residential-commercial districts. However, further analysis of the images does suggest that the type of commercial district in which the shelter is located does have implications for the success of the shelter. Many shelters in mixed residential and commercial districts, for example, were not located in communities with large box stores or high rise corporate office towers, but were in communities with small, locally managed businesses. The presence of these smaller community enterprises could have implications for the overall degree of community cohesion and sense of belongingness within a community. Further research – beyond the scope of the present book – would be helpful to clarify the implications of this finding. None of the shelter precedents we found to be successful existed within a heavy industrial zone, adjacent to a waste management (garbage) disposal or major utilities. Attention must be paid to conditions surrounding the shelter. For example, Image 3.9 illustrates the conditions across from the Good Shepherd Centre in Hamilton, Ontario (a shelter that provides dormitory lodgings for approximately sixty men). One can see from the picture that the community has been neglected. The adjacent and surrounding buildings have received no attention to their physical characteristics including upkeep and maintenance; this has direct implications for how this particular shelter is perceived in relation to the spatiality of the surrounding community.

Attention must be paid to the relationship between a shelter's physical location and the public realm. A shelter's connection with the broader public realm, particularly its immediate community, is vitally important. This manifests itself in all sorts of ways, including the nexus between private space and public space. For instance, city sidewalks and streets constitute a substantial portion of what could be considered the public realm. Parks and other landscapes are other examples of the public realm. Shelter design requires full consideration of the relationship between the shelter structure and the surrounding public realm. This may mean that shelters are designed such that clients are not required to lineup for services on the front sidewalks, or that shelters protect the privacy of their clientele by not posting large signs revealing their location on busy streets. But shelters are just one of many community members; other community members must also consider how their structures shape the public realm. For example, the image of the surrounding community presented in Image 3.9 illustrates the implications where other community members (property owners, developers, or city governments) ignore the importance of both maintaining structures and creating public realm space that is inviting.

If other members are not maintaining positive public realm space within communities, we believe shelters can take the lead. Image 3.10 of Centrepoint-Berwick Street in London, England (a shelter located in a mixed residential and commercial district that provides services to up to twenty-seven young men and/or women in single room occupancy suites) demonstrates the shelter's with full consideration to the public realm. The streetscape provides an avenue to limit the public awareness of a homeless shelter.

Image 3.7: Salvation Army Booth House, London

Image 3.8: Horizons for Youth, Toronto

Image 3.9: Good Shepherd Centre, Hamilton, Ontario

Image 3.10: Centrepoint – Berwick Street, London

Pictured in Image 3.11, The Fred Victor Mission in Toronto (which provides single room occupancy housing to 100+ people), likewise, presents a housing and shelter services centre across from a large green-space. Image 3.12 illustrates the shelter's consideration for the public realm. Notice that the sidewalk area is lined with bicycles and there is heavy motor-vehicle traffic throughout the street; thus the location of this facility is not intruding into the public realm. We are not suggesting that shelters need to be walled off and separated from the public realm. People accessing shelter services and staff and volunteers of the shelter should equally have the right to enjoy the offerings of the public realm. The distinction being made, though, is that the physical aspects of successful shelters do not redefine the use of the public realm surrounding the shelter to meet the programming needs of the shelter. Redefinitions of the public realm by the shelter can become a leading factor in redefining perceptions of communities and, may in turn, cause conflict within communities.

Similarly, Image 3.13 of the Endell Street Shelter in London, England presents a shelter above a row of local businesses. The public realm in this instance is not being influenced by the shelter's presence, as patrons of a local restaurant dine on a sidewalk patio.

Shelter Design

The physical design of a shelter is an equally important construct. Lefebvre (2000) characterizes space in a manner that highlights the significance of the subjective impressions held by people, since these impressions control what any given space represents. According to Hastings (2000), people should define space beyond its physical understanding and instead place emphasis on its subjective, socially constructed meanings.

When social service providers fail to address perceptions of the spatial condition in which they are located, they limit the ways in which people can positively engage with their environments (Landry, 2001; Worpole, 2000). The development of social housing projects in many Canadian cities – particularly of the era of the 1950s, 1960s, and 1970s – provides a clear example of this oversight (Rose, 1958). Many development initiatives, including those involving social housing, may pay little or no attention to the design and situation of their buildings (Gurney, 1999). Ironically, research has highlighted that many social housing problems are directly linked to how they, in the context of their surrounding neighborhoods, are perceived both by residents and other communities (Dean & Hastings, 2000; Hastings, 2000). Sadly, such research has had insufficient impact on many urban renewal discussions, particularly if the urban renewal process has predominantly been a

strategy utilized by government agencies to obtain land by eminent domain, demolish the structures on it, and then replan and redevelop the land for a different use (Kleniewski, 2002).

Changing the spatial perception of homelessness is a key factor to creating a socially and spatially inclusive environment for homeless individuals (Rosenthal, 2000). Here, both interior and exterior design are important. Regarding the interior, Friedman (1994) has contrasted *house* services, such as food, shelter, and accessibility to other services, and *home* services in which shelter services are provided in a welcoming, supportive environment. Having a home environment involves both physical shelter considerations and service delivery considerations. For example, a homeless shelter for youth may involve the opportunity to sit down family-style at a dining room table for a home-cooked meal. "Extras" like gas fireplaces or comfortable furniture also create a feeling of home.

Although future research could fruitfully analyze interior design characteristics of successful shelter service delivery, our focus us on the particular importance of exterior design. Image 3.14 and Image 3.15 provide examples of attention to the exterior design of shelters. The Bridges in Cambridge, Ontario (Image 3.14) is a mixed gender dormitory-style shelter in a mixed residential and commercial district. The Buffalo City Mission Women's Shelter in Buffalo, New York (Image 3.15) is in a mixed commercial and residential district and offers single room occupancy and dormitory services to upwards of 100 women and children.

These precedents illustrate the advantage of modern building materials that enhance the aesthetic character of the physical structure. Similarly, Image 3.16 of the Woodgreen Family and Child Centre in Toronto (a transitional housing apartment building for homeless women with children) presents a shelter that has considered the use of materials and overall design, but differs from the shelters in Images 3.14 and 3.15 because it also considers the characteristics of the surrounding community through its design: it was built at approximately the same height and style as the surrounding buildings. The importance of congruency will be explored further in the next section.

Shelter Size

A final consideration is physical size of the shelter building. There is much to be said for limiting the size of shelters, as large, monolithic shelters may not be appropriate in contrast with smaller scale approaches to service delivery. Yet the tendency to warehouse clients in large buildings is strong, and has the advantages of centralizing programs in a common location, which can be cost effective to deliver. Moreover, the problems of NIMBYism and

Precedent Research

Image 3.15: Buffalo City Women's Shelter, Buffalo, New York

Image 3.16: The Woodgreen Family & Childcare Centre

the sheer economy of shelter acquisition, building, and administration may preclude approaches other than warehousing. Our research discovered evidence that the physical size of a shelter is not solely connected to a shelter's success. Shelters analyzed for the purposes of this research were both spatially large and small. For example, Image 3.17 illustrates Coops Foyer in Manchester, England and Image 3.18 illustrates The Times Square Hotel in New York; both are low cost, affordable housing projects with a mix of spaces (i.e. single room occupancy or single bedroom apartment suites).

In contrast, Image 3.19 is of a small service organization with programs for people experiencing homelessness in downtown Vancouver. The red brick building in the forefront of the picture is called the Gathering Place and provides community and recreational resources during the day for some of the homeless population in Vancouver. Other resource centres, in contrast, are physically large. One such example is the Austin Resource Center for the Homeless (ARCH) in Austin, Texas (Image 3.20).

Both large and small shelters and service delivery centres can be successful within urban landscapes. As with shelter design, always and everywhere, a shelter's scale is in relation to the broader community in which it is situated.

Image 3.18: Times Square Hotel, New York

Image 3.19: The Gathering Place, Vancouver

Shelter Integration

The previous discussion illustrates physical dimensions of shelters that have been identified as successful. There is a connection between those physical features and the overall integration of the shelter within its surrounding community. Three sub-themes emerge: congruency with the surrounding community, private programming spaces, and community dynamics. Each is discussed in turn.

Congruency with the Surrounding Community

The idea of community is in large part subjective; in and out of a spatial/physical context, it has a lot to do with the nature and quality of social interactions. Such ethereal concepts as "sense of community" may be nonetheless accessible. They result from acts of support between community members, personal attachment to a particular place, and strong social ties (Skjaeveland, Garling, & Maeland, 1996). Being neighborly is based primarily on an individual's degree of alienation or non-alienation from others in the community, belongingness and the quality of life within the community, as well as the level of care that a person has for the community and/or others in the community (Hughey & Bardo, 1984). Social capital is important to the nature and quality of interactions between community members (Unger & Wandersman, 1982). By social capital, we mean networks of associations, the active and willing engagement in a community, and a sense of trust and common social norms with others (Coleman, 1988; Putnam, 2000). Social capital is based partly on peoples' historical connection to a particular area, their overall general quality of life, and their satisfaction with the community. A neighborhood and community – as a physical place and as a source of social relationships – are key to social capital and mutually reinforce it. In fact, some contend that community cohesion can be measured by defining both social relationships and the physical history of a neighborhood (Riger & Lavrakas, 1981).

Our research leads us to believe that a sense of commitment and care in a community, and the built environment of a shelter, interact and can facilitate improved interactions between community members. This can mean the shelter as a community member, or the guests of the shelter service as community members. Image 3.21 of Endsleigh Gardens in London, England (a hostel for a mix of people experiencing homelessness) provides one such example of this commitment and care in relation to the shelter's appearance, hence contributing to the community's acceptance of the shelter.

Image 3.20: Austin Resource Center for the Homeless

Image 3.21: Endleigh Gardens Shelter, London

The shelter in Image 3.21 exists in an older community, and the architectural form of the building resembles the historical era in which it was built. Similar examples can be found elsewhere: The Times Square Hotel in Image 3.18 above, for example, has a similar function historically, but is now housing individuals in a new capacity. In contrast, Image 3.22 is of the Union Gospel Mission in an older community, but the structure and physical size of the shelter is not consistent with the surrounding community. The Union Gospel Mission in Vancouver, British Columbia provides single room occupancy housing services to thirty-six men. The shelter is small, but the visibility of the shelter within that community is more pronounced, and as a result may contribute to a negative perception of the shelter within a community.

In contrast, The Franciscan Center (Image 3.23) in Buffalo, New York is an example of a shelter located in an older residential community that maintains congruency with the built environment characteristics of the surrounding residences. This shelter offers dormitory lodging for up to 6 youth. The Franciscan Center has visible signage out front: in this way, some shelters are quite visible, others less so, and others not at all. The signage was not identified by this particular shelter's staff as impacting the shelter's ability to maintain community congruency. Yet, for some shelters, not having signage is beneficial; limiting the physical presence of the shelter in the community, and protecting the confidentiality of their residents. Shelters make signage choices based on their need to be visible to clients versus their need to be more discrete, sometimes for the safety of residents.

Image 3.24 is the same shelter depicted in Image 3.16 above (The Woodgreen Family and Child Centre). It is a further example of how a shelter can maintain congruency within communities through design choices. Images 3.25 and 3.26 also demonstrate this point. Image 3.25 is of the Rachel Women's Center in San Diego, California; women are not housed within the drop-in centre but across the street in the top floor of a US post office building. There, up to thirty-five women are provided single room occupancy lodging. Image 3.26 is of the Larkin Street Youth Services Center in San Francisco, California, which provides housing and educational support for street youth. Successful shelters range in sizes physically and also in regard to the number of people in which service is provided at any given time. Their impact and subsequent relationship with the surrounding community is based on their ability to "fit in".

The following image of Huckleberry House, a residential youth shelter in San Francisco, California and the surrounding neighborhood (Image 3.27) further illustrates shelter congruency with the community. In one of these images there is a shelter. Other examples of congruency can be found within our data set: for example Naomi House (Image 3.28) in St. John's, Newfoundland and Adsum House (Image 3.29) in Halifax, Nova Scotia.

Image 3.22: Union Gospel Mission, Vancouver

Image 3.23: Franciscan Center, Buffalo, New York

Image 3.26: Larkin Street Youth Services, San Francisco

Image 3.27: Huckleberry House, San Francisco

Image 3.28: Naomi House, St. John's, Newfoundland

Image 3.29: Adsum House, Halifax, Nova Scotia

A shelter's ability to fit in is also based on the historical use of the chosen building within a neighborhood: is the building being used for a similar or complementary purpose as it has historically been used? For example, The Christopher in New York, a 207 unit supportive housing residence in Manhattan (Image 3.30), was formerly YMCA housing. Similarly, the Atlanta Children's Shelter, which provides day shelter to homeless children and family support services in Atlanta, Georgia (Image 3.31) is located within an historical church building.

Image 3.30: The Christopher, New York

Programming Location

A shelter's integration in a community is also influenced by the area in which its programs are offered. Location of programming is part of a broader discussion of what constitutes, or should constitute, the public realm. Many of the shelters presented here have been able to integrate within communities by maintaining programs only within shelter property. For many activities, whether it is to get into the cinema or a restaurant, line-ups typically happen on public space (sidewalks etc.) or in view from public space. Line-ups also may also be required to secure residence or meals at a shelter. To avoid commensurate intrusion into public spaces, some shelters had gathering space for guests to congregate and socialize (Image 3.32 and Image 3.33). Image 3.32 is of an interior courtyard at the San Diego Rescue Mission, a shelter providing services to upwards of seventy women and children in a mix of dormitory and single room occupancy shelter spaces. Image 3.33 is of the Lookout Downtown Hazelton Residence in Vancouver, British Columbia. This facility offers a transitional/supportive housing in a building with thirty-nine suites.

The integration of public space within the shelter's environment has implications for quality of service delivery. Privacy for guests of these shelters is a primary component of dignified and respectful service. Images 3.34 and 3.35 both demonstrate the role of the built environment in promoting privacy through the location of entryways and exits from the shelter. Image 3.34 is of the Good Shepherd Family Centre in Hamilton, Ontario. The centre is located in a residential district and offers shelter accommodations for families. In contrast, Image 3.35 is of Good Shepherd Centre in Hamilton, which provides dormitory style shelter services to upwards of sixty men.

Community Dynamics

Many shelters are in high traffic areas. The Bowery Mission in New York (Image 3.36), which provides dormitory style shelter services to sixty men, is a prime example of such shelters. This provides insight into the relevance of sidewalk traffic for a shelter's dynamic with the community. For example, if there is a high volume of public sidewalk traffic, the homeless may be more integrated within the public realm and less likely to be the target of public scrutiny. We suspect that those who are not homeless may be less fearful or intimated by the homeless in these high volume areas compared to open, barren streetscapes where there are many homeless and few non-homeless. Many of the images demonstrate the vibrancy around these shelters. Vibrant

Image 3.34: Good Shepherd Family Centre, Hamilton

Image 3.35: Good Shepherd Centre, Hamilton, Ontario

Image 3.36: The Bowery Mission, New York

public spaces also make it less likely that homeless individuals are targeted for violence. Image 3.37 taken in New York outside the Prince George Hotel (a low-income apartment similar to the Times Square Hotel described above), provides one such example of this phenomenon. These shelters, like many presented in the images above, are responsive to the dynamics of the community in which they are located.

Image 3.37: Streetscape near low-income apartment, New York

Conclusion – Built Environment Impact on Service Delivery

Homelessness service delivery should be tailored to meet the needs of different populations (Hertlein & Killmer, 2004). Services may be more effective when they specialize in a particular population, rather than attempting to provide services for a broad range of homeless individuals. For example, this might encompass particular service models for homeless individuals who have substance addictions, or homeless individuals who have suffered domestic violence.

In the past, some scholars have considered shelter services in Canada as consisting of both *traditional* and *alternative* type (O'Reilly-Fleming, (1993). This typology remains a useful overall template to consider services, even though some overlaps occur between types and both models can sometimes coexist in the same shelter service. The typology holds that traditional shelter models make clients ultimately responsible for re-entry into the population of the housed and employed. Traditional service may include large institutional settings for male patrons providing lodging to hundreds of people per night, shelters with religious affiliations for men, shelters or hostels specifically for women between the ages of sixteen to twenty-four, shelters that act as cooperatives for adolescents, and shelters and hostels for women and children. Also, for those who are physically able to work, employment may be considered key to becoming housed; once an individual is integrated in the labor market there should be little need for further intervention. Interventions may be necessary in terms of ongoing support if addictions or mental health issues are a concern. However, in cases where market rent is not achievable through a minimum wage, there is a structural problem that requires attention from institutional and government levels.

Alternative shelter types hold that people have diverse needs and thus require diversified service models and levels of support to establish permanent residency. These may include shelters for abused women and their children, extended stay residential apartment units for men, motel conversions specifically for families with children. Additionally, shelters need to be responsive and sensitive to cultural and spiritual practices of specific populations such as Aboriginal people (Walsh, Rutherford, & Kusmak, in press). The former Streetcity warehouse-style shelter in Toronto provides an illustrative example of the conversion to an alternative model in the Canadian context (Anderson, 1998). The Streetcity shelter was shut down in 2003 and transformed into an alternative facility known as Strachan House (Bridgman, 2006). There were several examples of alternative shelter types within this research, including transitional housing models like the Fred Victor Mission in Toronto and the Massey Centre for Women in Toronto, located in a residential neighborhood providing housing and other related services to seventy-six women and children in single room occupancy suites, single bedroom apartments, and townhouses. While shelters presented throughout this analysis are primarily alternative shelter types, the findings have implications for all types of shelter.

It may be difficult for shelter management to consider all above mentioned characteristics. However, it is possible to expand, change, or implement new features in shelter design or service delivery to improve the current shelter. Images 3.38 and 3.39 are additional illustrations of the Franciscan Center (Image 3.23), and demonstrate the role of the built environment in facilitating successful expansion of this shelter service model. The further development (Image 3.38) of this shelter improved spatial

factors like exterior design but maintained congruency with the surrounding community (Image 3.39). This shelter also had a size and scale that was aligned with the dynamics of the community.

Our research has implications for human service practitioners and urban planners in their continued attempts to promote social inclusion of marginalized populations and to promote community cohesion between residences, social services, and businesses. A primary finding is that no single model of service delivery or physical design is appropriate across all communities. What works in one community may not be as effective or appropriate in another; what effectively serves one population may be inadequate to meet the needs of another. Thus, consideration of the role of the built environment is highly important to the effectiveness and success of a shelter, both in consideration of the needs of the clientele and the needs of the broader community. This chapter illustrates characteristics of the built environment for homeless shelter service delivery models. But there are limitations to the findings. For example, we do not know how these built environment characteristics change community member perceptions. Further research could explore questions related to the construction of positive or negative community perceptions of homeless shelters. Chapter Four presents some conclusions regarding the design of our case study example in Chapter Two, as well as the broader considerations of urban design in Chapter Three.

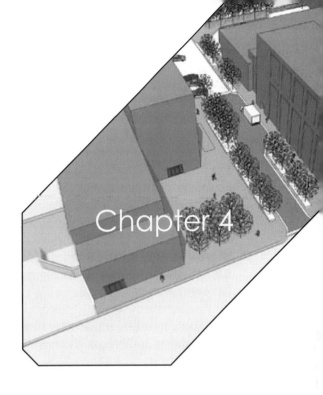

Chapter 4

Conclusion

Social service organizations are challenged by their physical environments to promote social justice and provide dignified and respectable services to their client populations. Homelessness and shelter service delivery provide strong evidence of these challenges. As discussed in earlier chapters, homelessness itself is deeply entrenched in the physical realm, and service delivery (i.e. shelters and other services) for those people experiencing homelessness is, in many ways, interwoven with discussions of spatiality within an urban context. Homelessness is often overlooked in the development process; an "out of sight, out of mind" approach may very quickly turn already marginalized people into a social and business liability that is segregated and isolated from the wider community. This research has helped foster more constructive perceptions of homeless shelters and the role they play in the community.

Little research identifies solutions to promote interconnectedness between the physical and social realm. Social work emphasizes the person in their immediate social environment; social issues and their manifestations in the individual, family, or community are seen to be a result of the interplay between the person and social environment factors. As Chapter One points out, the social situation of being without a home and requiring the use of shelter services is associated with other social conditions external to the individual. Factors related to the social environment such as poverty or the absence of adequate housing stock may lead to homelessness. The methods of improving these conditions should be of utmost concern.

Amongst advanced industrialized countries, surely the end of homelessness should be a priority, especially considering adequate housing is a universal human right. Our research addresses service delivery systems that help to improve the social environment experiences of people who are without permanent housing. To improve these social environment experiences, though, as this research has demonstrated, research and education needs to move beyond the narrow understanding of what impacts a person's social environment. An approach that also examines the conditions within the physical realm that influence the social environment experiences – such as isolation, segregation, scrutiny, and/or marginalization, among others – is required.

A growing wave of environmental design scholarship documents the need for further consideration of social environment experiences in urban planning. This environmental design literature does not address adequately the relationship between the built environment and social service programs. Equally, minimal social work and social science scholarship appraises the implications of the physical environment on populations receiving services (Weeks, 2004). Some scholarship has considered the implications of the physical environment in relation to client experiences when receiving service. For example, research has examined characteristics of the immediate physical space in which the service is provided: the location or proximity of chairs in a counseling session, or structural considerations required to accommodate people in wheelchairs (see Breton, 1984; Griffin, Mauritzen, & Kasmer, 1969; Gutheil, 1992; Kahn & Scher, 2002; Nicotera, 2005; Resnick & Jaffee, 1982; Walz, Willenbring, & Demoll, 1974). The physical realm also requires consideration with respect to the macrostructural issues that profoundly impact homelessness.

Positive social service delivery models can be created in part by a careful consideration of the role of the built environment. As noted in Chapter Three, it is possible to integrate shelters within communities in ways that benefit all members of the community. This final chapter draws on the findings of this research with a primary focus first on its application to the physical situation of the Mustard Seed Street Ministry in Calgary, Alberta, followed by a more general discussion of the applicability of the findings from this research to other urban centres and shelter services.

The Mustard Seed and Surrounding Physical Environment

The Mustard Seed has the potential to influence the social dynamic of the surrounding area and to set a precedent for the urban quality of future development. There are several opportunities for this to happen. By establishing a high quality public space node, the Mustard Seed defines the corner of the Centre Street S. and 11th Avenue S. intersection (see Image 2.9). Future development in the area can continue the trend of infilling the block, reducing *lost space* (space that does not presently serve a positive functional or visual role) and thereby creating a vibrant streetscape. From a social standpoint, the Seed expansion will be the first of its kind in Calgary, and can act as an example for dealing with agency integration within this city and in other parts of the country and throughout North America and Europe. Further research post-development would be useful to analyze the implications of such an approach.

There are immediate physical assets surrounding the Mustard Seed Street Ministry, including two lots of land along 11th Avenue, which are currently used for parking. These are areas that could quickly be developed, given the current economic climate in Calgary, to both help define the street and work towards making the area around the Seed an interesting and inviting area for all people. There are also constraints within the physical environment that hinder, from an environmental design perspective, the creation of a better streetscape, including the Canada Pacific Railway tracks, the infrequent railway underpasses, and the massive building blocks that spatially limit the interaction between the site and the northern half of downtown. The scale and impermeability of the parking garages in the Calgary Tower block and the poor quality of most of the streetscape do not seem to consider the importance of the public realm, and many of the approved development plans and projects under construction have not considered the Mustard Seed in their long-term vision of the area.

Spatial and social principles include objectives that could be applied to a redevelopment/expansion model of the Mustard Seed Street Ministry site:

- The provision of shade and shelter for guests and the public.
- The creation of high-quality public space between buildings as programmable gathering space.
- The development of a safe and legible pedestrian environment.
- A shelter entrance which serves to reduce vehicle/pedestrian conflicts on Centre Street.
- The availability of adequate parking for Mustard Seed operations.
- Necessary improvements to the streetscape along all roadways (10th and 11th avenues and Centre Street) adjacent to the shelter building(s).
- Increase in the visual quality and character (of the building and surrounding area) to improve public perceptions.
- Building additions to the shelter's physical structure (shown in the following diagrams of conceptual alternatives).

Conceptual alternatives for the Mustard Seed Street Ministry were also informed by five distinct design principles:

- All developments should include active uses along the street edge (including retail outlets).
- Visual permeability should exist between indoor and outdoor through the use of windows.
- Multiple entries should be included to contribute to vibrancy.
- All developments should consider incorporating elements that respond to human scale (a scale consistent with that of a human being). For example, elements of consideration for buildings include keeping sight lines open and providing adequate lighting.
- All developments should aim for a mix of uses and a mix of housing types to avoid the formation of single-use areas or of low-income housing ghettos.

Conceptual Alternatives for the Mustard Seed

The urban design concepts for the development of the Mustard Seed outlined on the following pages are divided into two design alternatives, each following two potential scenarios: 1) maintaining the strip-mall building on the site's northeast corner, and 2) building a new structure on the site.

In Alternative A, the alley behind the Mustard Seed building has been closed off, creating a semi-private outdoor area under the agency's jurisdiction. A four-storey structure has been added to the north end of the Creative Centre, and the south edge of this building has been brought to the street edge with strong potential for the development of commercial space. Centre Street has been redesignated to one-way vehicular traffic northbound, and the street has been narrowed. A selection of traffic-calming devices, including on-street parking, bollards, acute turns, raised crosswalks, and textured surfaces all ensure a safer relationship between pedestrian and vehicle on this shared space. A human-scale plaza has been established in front of the Creative Centre, providing a comfortable pedestrian environment for all citizens and a variety of outdoor programming opportunities for the Mustard Seed. Improvements in the quality of the street environment throughout the block include higher-quality surfaces and a substantial increase in the presence of street trees.

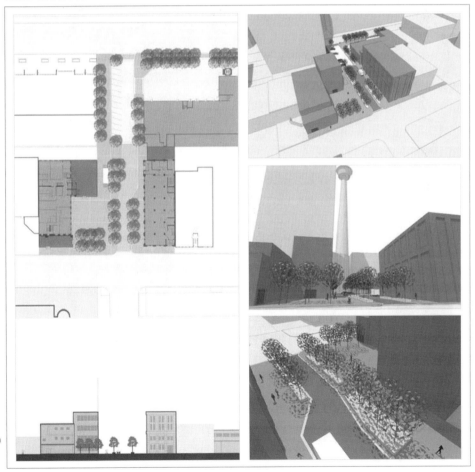

Image 4.1

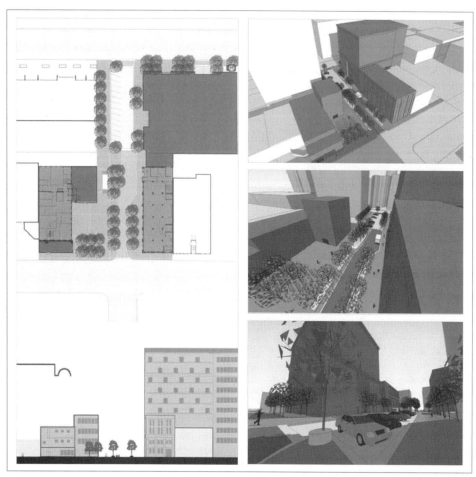

Alternative B is similar to Alternative A in many ways, but it differs in two respects. First, the alley that is closed off in Alternative A remains open in this second iteration. This allows for the negotiation of a balance between building connectivity, pedestrian safety, and service access, and depends on a variety of practical and legislative restrictions. The other major difference in Alternative B is that the retail frontage on the south end of the Creative Centre has been extended east into the public space. The alternative redevelopment models have been presented here to account for a negotiation between the volume of retail space required, the degree of definition of the public plaza, and the amount of sunlight access into the public plaza, all of which depend on constraints yet unknown.

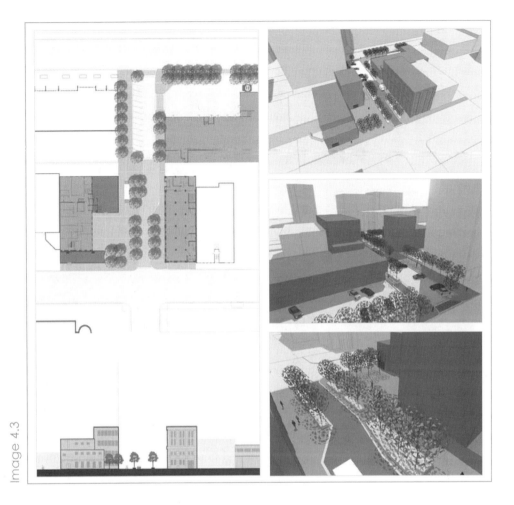

Image 4.3

Summary and Recommendations for the Mustard Seed

The Mustard Seed's longstanding role as a service provider within Calgary and the immediate neighborhood in which it is located should be celebrated and maintained. Through the built environment, this research has demonstrated that there are a number of strategies that The Mustard Seed can employ to better serve clients and maintain positive interactions with the surrounding neighborhood:

- The Mustard Seed management might consider the construction of a courtyard to avoid line-ups in and around the area that may serve to negatively impact client dignity and may contribute to negative perceptions of the area by other members of the community.

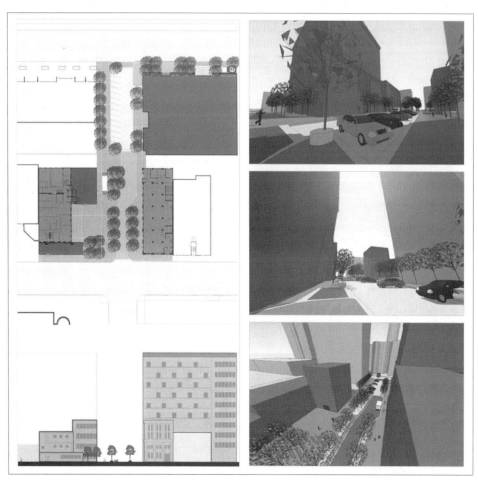

- Further landscaping including trees and green spaces could improve the visual appeal of the area and will help make clients feel they are entitled to free use of the area. Mustard Seed clients could help in the construction and maintenance of public spaces to be used as daytime gathering places; this could instill a sense of ownership and pride in those using them and provide meaningful employment.
- The Mustard Seed's services include programming such as education and employment training, and further development or improvements to this programming, particularly in regards to new equipment or expansion of programs, would be beneficial for clientele. Some of the Seed's programs have potential for store-front retail outlets, which would add to the vibrancy of the street while providing revenue.
- Mustard Seed management could consider the construction of more discreet entrances to help guests feel at ease, especially for those who

have experienced anxiety or discrimination accessing shelter services in a public manner.

- The Mustard Seed Ministry can improve interactions with the community by asking for input and working with residents in regards to improvements that can be made to the shelter. Community support and input may help to improve relationships and reduce hostility between homeless citizens and the surrounding community.
- There is a need for more accessible public washrooms in many areas of the inner city. Providing washrooms that are truly accessible by everyone will improve not only this needed service for homeless citizens but will also increase their sense of dignity while fostering better relationships with the public.
- The Mustard Seed buildings should retain their current scale and size in order to blend well into the surrounding urban context. There are currently some development scenarios being contemplated by the Mustard Seed for the development of a twenty-seven-storey tower that would provide temporary shelter for homeless people as well as affordable and longer-term transitional housing. The scale of this proposal may have a negative effect on the neighborhood, may contribute to negative community perceptions, and may further concentrate and marginalize its users. If the tower is constructed, then particular care needs to be taken to ensure that the ground levels have a strong interface with the sidewalk, and provide a mix of uses that includes retail uses for a broader population than just Mustard Seed guests. If this does not occur, then there is a dangerous potential that the street facade of the tower will become even more of a negatively perceived block.
- The Mustard Seed's location allows guests to not only access the services that the shelter provides but is also in close proximity to other essential services such as medical clinics and donation sites, and its downtown location means public transportation is easily accessible to clients. This is a significant asset and should be recognized in any development concepts for the area.

Shelter Services Beyond Calgary

The results of this research expand the knowledge of how the built environment impacts service delivery of social programs. Furthermore, the results help frame practical considerations that could be taken by urban planners, policy makers, land developers, and a multitude of other individuals to formulate an improved understanding of the relationship between shelter design and service delivery frameworks. Recommendations for the Mustard Seed Street Ministry have been formulated based on the analysis of data collected through the precedent research (see Chapter Three) in comparison and relation to the present physical situation of the Mustard Seed in Calgary (see Chapter Two). An underlying requirement of these recommendations is an understanding of the local contexts within which homeless shelters are situated and their daily operations occur. Thus, this research does have implications for shelter services in other urban contexts within cities throughout North America and Europe, where contexts and therefore recommendations may be both similar and different, but understanding this context is key.

Shelter success can be identified as the ability of a shelter to meet the immediate needs and long-term goals of those people accessing the service. Some scholars categorize goals based on outcomes such as the ability to secure stable housing (see Glisson, Thyer, & Fischer, 2001), while others measure success based on the ability of the shelter service system to challenge structural factors leading to homelessness (see Culhane, 1992). Ideology and worldview contribute to definitions of success. The findings of this research suggest that a shelter is successful if the interrelationships between service delivery, the broader community, and the built environment are all considered. Within service delivery, education and employment programming, *home* rather than merely *house* services, and attention to client dignity and safety were some factors we conclude improve shelter success. Regarding the broader community, challenging negative perceptions of homeless people, collaborating with stakeholders, and creating possibilities for positive community engagement with the shelter and its residents, can all be methods of reducing problems in the shelter's community. Reflecting on factors of the built environment is likely to produce positive results if they are incorporated into planning. These factors include spatiality, or what is happening around the shelter (location, sidewalks, landscaping, small businesses), features of design such as the use of modern materials, and shelter congruency and size. This research has clarified the ways in which these three broad elements interact to affect the issue of homelessness in either positive or negative ways. Aspects of the built environment can influence the shelter service system, which in turn may have negative implications for community relationships. For example, the use of design features such as interior courtyards may say something about a shelter's attention to client dignity and may have a direct impact on a shelter's relationship with its surrounding community. Good design features must be methodically planned in collaboration with community partners with due regard given to the shelter's particular context. In sum, service delivery organizations can respond to the challenges they face through the implementation of some of these physical realm considerations in the design and function of their shelter.

This research has not provided an overview of what a shelter should be. In fact, shelter services need to differ from one community to the next, from one population of service users to the next, and within one policy jurisdiction to the next. There is no concrete answer to what a shelter is to look like or what services are to be like in absolute terms. Instead, careful reflection on the above topics should be undertaken as a collaborative community effort. Rather than provide broadly generic suggestions for shelter design, perhaps it would be useful to consider the following questions:

- What population will this shelter serve?
- What special needs of this population should be taken into account regarding shelter design, and/or location?
- What other shelters serve this population, and what can you learn from them prior to constructing the shelter?
- Is protecting the clients' identity going to be particularly important? What features can we implement to ensure this is done?
- In fully helping this population, what kinds of programs will be offered? If the shelter is already in existence, how can we improve the programs that are currently offered?
- What kinds of design attributes can we use to ensure client dignity and safety, to the best of our ability?
- What kinds of design mechanisms would make this building feel more like a *home* than a *shelter*?
- Describe what is happening in the area of the proposed location.
- What kinds of people live in the area? What do you think their perceptions of homeless people are?
- How can we improve the surrounding area in building this shelter (i.e. landscaping, improved sidewalks, green space etc.)?
- Have you consulted with the community? If not, are there currently opportunities to collaborate and engage the community prior to building the shelter (i.e. community meetings, condo board meetings etc.)?
- Are there other services or commercial outlets in the area? What kinds of services or commercial outlets? Will these be beneficial for our clientele?
- Is the location close to transit?
- Does the location have a mix of uses, buildings, and people?
- Describe the surrounding buildings. How big are they? What materials were used in constructing them?
- If you are renovating an old building, what prior use did it have, and is this use similar to a shelter?
- What are the most important results you hope to achieve with the construction of this shelter? How can you best achieve those, particularly with attention to design?

This list of questions is by no means exhaustive, but each of these questions reflects one of the three broader factors of service delivery, community relationships and the built environment. We hope this will be a useful tool in understanding the best possible shelter design for your community.

An underlying assumption of this research is that improvements in the built environment have a positive impact on community perceptions of homelessness and shelter services. In this research, positive community perception was garnered from interviews with shelter operators who described minimal or absent community opposition to some of these successful precedents. Furthermore, the presence of positive community perceptions of shelters was demonstrated by the level of social interactions and public realm access immediately surrounding the shelters in many of these communities. Further research could contribute to further understanding the perceptions of community members within the immediate locality of shelters, to gaining insight into the perceptions the homeless individuals accessing shelter precedents, and to exploring the impact of characteristics of a shelter's interior environment on service delivery.

References

Anderson, R. (1998). Street as metaphor in housing for the homeless. *Journal of Social Distress and The Homeless, 6*(1), 1-12.

Bentley, I., Alcock, A., McGlynn, S., Murrain, P., & Smith G. (1985). *Responsive environments: A manual for designers*. London: The Architectural Press.

Breton, M. (1984). A drop-in program for transient women: Promoting competence through the environment. *Social Work, 29*(6), 542-546.

Bridgman, R. (2006). *StreetCities: Rehousing the homeless*. Toronto: Broadview Press.

CBC. (April 23, 2008). *Off the streets*. Retrieved on June 6, 2008 from: http://www.cbc.ca/national/blog/video/healtheducation/off_the_streets_ 1.html

City of Calgary Planning Advisory Committee. (1966). *The future of downtown Calgary*. Calgary: City of Calgary.

Cloke, P., Widdowfield, R., & Milbourne, P. (2000). Homelessness and rurality: Out of place in purified space. *Environment and Planning, Society, and Space, 18*, 715-735.

Coleman, J. S. (1988). Social capital in the creation of human capital. *American Journal of Sociology, 94*, s95- s120.

Cox, K. (1997). Governance, urban regime analysis, and the politics of local economic development. In M. Lauria (Ed.), *Regulating urban politics in a global economy* (pp. 99-121). Thousand Oaks: Sage Publications.

Culhane, D. P. (1992). The quandaries of shelter reform: An appraisal of efforts to "manage" homelessness. *Social Service Review, 63*(3), 428-440.

Davis, M. (1990). *City of quartz*. London: Verso.

Dean, J. & Hastings, A. (2000). *Challenging images: Housing estates, stigma and regeneration*. York: Policy Press.

Dear, M. & Wolch, J. (1987). *Landscapes of despair: From deinstitutionalization to homelessness*. Princeton: Princeton University Press.

Despres, C. (1991). The meaning of home: Literature review and directions for future research and theoretical development. *Journal of Architectural and Planning Research, 8*(2), 96-114.

DeVerteuil, G. (2006). The local state of homeless shelters: Beyond revanchism? *Cities, 23*(2), 109-120.

Ellin, N. (1996). *Postmodern urbanism*. Oxford: Blackwell Publishers.

Fink, P. J. & Tasman, A. (1992). *Stigma and mental illness*. Washington: American Psychiatric Press.

Fitzpatrick, S., Kemp, P., & Klinker, S. (2000). *Single homelessness: An overview of research in Britain*. Bristol, UK: The Policy Press.

Freeman, L. & Braconi, F. (2004). Gentrification and displacement: New York in the 1990's. *Journal of the American Planning Association, 70*, 39-52.

Friedman, B. D. (1994). No place like home: A study of two homeless shelters. *Journal of Social Distress and the Homeless, 3*(4), 321-339.

Galabuzi, G. E. (2008). Social exclusion: Socio-economic and political implications of the racialized gap. In M. A. Wallis & S. Kwok (Eds.), *Daily struggles: The deepening racialization and feminization of poverty in Canada* (pp. 81-93). Toronto: Canadian Scholars' Press.

Galbraith, J. K. (1958). *The affluent society*. New York: Mariner Books.

Glisson, G. M., Thyer, B. A., & Fischer, R. L. (2001). Serving the homeless:Evaluating the effectiveness of homeless shelter services. *Journal of Sociology and Social Welfare, 28*(4), 89-97.

Graham, J. R. (2007, November 1). More than just bricks and mortar. *Calgary Herald*, A16.

Graham, J. R. (1995). Lessons for today: Canadian municipalities and unemployment relief during the 1930s Great Depression. *Canadian Review of Social Policy, 35*, 1-18.

Graham, J. R., & Kuiken, J. (2007, June 8). Seed tower must not be an urban ghetto. *Calgary Herald*, A25.

Graham, J. R., Swift, K., & Delaney, R. (2008). *Canadian social policy: An introduction* (3rd ed.). Toronto: Prentice Hall.

Greer, N. R. (1986). *The search for shelter*. Washington D.C.: The American Institute of Architects.

Griffin, W. V., Mauritzen, J. H., & Kasmar, J. V. (1969). The psychological aspects of the architectural environment: A review. *American Journal of Psychiatry, 125*(8), 1057-1062.

Gurney, C. (1999). Lowering the drawbridge: A case study of analogy and metaphor in the social construction of home ownership. *Urban Studies, 36*(1), 1705-1722.

Gutheil, I. A. (1992). Considering the physical environment: An essential component of good practice. *Social Work, 37*(5), 391-396.

Hareven, T. K. (1991). The home and the family in historical perspective. *Social Research, 58*(1), 253-285.

Hartman, C. (1979). Comment on 'Neighborhood revitalization and displacement: A review of the evidence'. *American Planning Association Journal, 45*, 488-491.

Hartnett, H. P. & Harding, S. (2005). Geography and shelter: Implications for community practice with people experiencing homelessness. *Journal of Progressive Human Sciences, 16*(2), 25-46.

Hastings, A. (2000). Discourse analysis: What does it offer housing studies? *Housing Theory and Society, 17*, 131-139.

Hayden, D. (1982). *The grand domestic revolution: A history of feminist designs for American homes, neighborhoods, and cities.* Cambridge, MA: MIT Press.

Herman, J. (1992). *Trauma and recovery: The aftermath of violence.* New York: Basic Books.

Hertlein, K. M. & Killmer, J. M. (2004). Toward differentiated decision-making: Family systems theory with the homeless clinical population. *The American Journal of Family Therapy, 32*(3), 255-270.

Hill, P. R. (1985). The world their household: The American woman's foreign mission movement and cultural transformation, 1870-1920. Ann Arbor: University of Michigan Press.

Hiller, H. H. & Moylan, D. (1999) Mega-events and community obsolescence: Redevelopment versus rehabilitation in Victoria Park East. *Canadian Journal of Urban Research, 8*, 47-81.

Hocking, J. E. & Lawrence, S. G. (2000). Changing attitudes toward the homeless: The effects of prosocial communication with the homeless. *Journal of Social Distress and the Homeless, 9*, 91-110.

Hough, M. (1990). Out of place: Restoring identity to the regional landscape. New Haven, CT: Yale University Press

Hughey, J. B. & Bardo, J. W. (1984). The structure of community satisfaction in a southeastern American city. *The Journal of Social Psychology, 123*, 91-99.

Ismael, S. (2006). *Child poverty and the Canadian welfare state: From entitlement to charity.* Edmonton: University of Alberta Press.

Jacobs, J. (1961). *The death and life of great American cities.* New York: Random House.

Jacobs, K. (2002). Subjectivity and the transformation of urban spatial experience. *Housing Theory And Society, 19*, 102-111.

Kahn, M. & Scher, S. (2002). Infusing content on the physical environment into the BSW curriculum. *The Journal of Baccalaureate Social Work, 7*(2), 1-14.

Katz, M. (1975). *The people of Hamilton, Canada West: Family and class in a mid-nineteenth century city.* Cambridge, MA: Harvard University Press.

Keiller, P. (1998). The dilapidated dwelling. *Architectural Design, 134,* 22-27.

Kennedy, C. & Fitzpatrick, S. (2001). Begging, rough sleeping, and social exclusion: Implications for social policy. *Urban Studies, 38*(11), 2001-2016.

Kennett, P. (1994). Modes of regulation of the urban poor. *Urban Studies, 31*(7), 1017-1031.

Kingwell, M. (2000). *The world we want.* New York: Viking Press.

Kleniewski, N. (2002). *Cities, change and conflict: A political economy of urban life.* Toronto: Nelson Thomson Learning.

Laaksonen, M., Martikainen, P., Nihtilä, E., Rahkonen O., & Lahelma, E. (2008). Homeownership and mortality: A register-based follow up study of 300 000 Finns. *Community Health, 62,* 293-297.

Laird, G. (2007). *Homelessness in a growth economy: Canada's 21st century paradox.* Calgary: Sheldon Chumir Foundation for Ethics in Leadership.

Landry, C. (2001). The creative city: Harnessing people's imagination. *Streetwise, 42,* 2-7.

Lasch, C. (1975). *Haven in a heartless world: The family besieged.* New York: Basic Books.

Lefebvre, H. (2000). *The production of space.* Oxford: Blackwell Publishing.

Ley, D. (1996). *The new middle class and the remaking of the central city.* New York: Oxford University Press.

Lindblom, E. N. (1991) Towards a comprehensive homelessness-prevention strategy. *Housing Policy Debate, 2*(3), 957-1025.

Lobao, L. M, Hooks, G., & Tickamyer, A. R. (2007). *The sociology of spatial inequality.* Albany, NY: State University of New York Press.

Lynch, K. (1960). *The image of the city.* Cambridge, MA: MIT Press.

Lynch, K. (1976). *Managing the sense of a region.* Cambridge, MA: MIT Press.

Lynch, K. (1981) *A theory of good city form.* Cambridge, MA: MIT Press.

Marcuse, P. (1988). Neutralizing homelessness. *Socialist Review, 18*(1), 69-96.

McLeod, G. (2002). From urban entrepreneurialism to a revanchist city: On the spatial injustices of Glasgow's renaissance. *Antipode, 34,* 602-624.

Mitchell, D. (1997). The annihilation of space bylaw: The roots and implications of anti-homeless laws in the United States. *Antipode, 29,* 303-336.

Mohan, J. (2002). Geographies of welfare and social exclusion: Dimensions, consequences, and methods. *Progress in Human Geography, 26*(1), 45-75.

Morgenstern, C. (1918). *Stages: A development in aphorisms and diary notes.* Munich: R. Piper & Co.

Murphy, B. (2000). *On the street: How we created the homeless*. Toronto: J. Gordon Publishing.

Nicotera, N. (2005). The child's view of neighborhood: Assessing a neglected element in direct social work practice. *Journal of Human Behavior in the Social Environment, 11*(3/4), 105-133.

O'Reilly-Fleming, T. (1993). *Down and out in Canada: Homeless Canadians*. Toronto: Canadian Scholars' Press.

Paterson, D., et al. (1994). Regionalism reconsidered. *Forum, Landscape Architecture, 84*(4), 70-74.

Pleace, N. (1998). Single homeless as social exclusion: The unique and the extreme. *Social Policy and Administration, 32*(1), 46- 59.

Putnam, R. D. (2000). *Bowling alone: The collapse and revival of American community*. New York: Simon and Schuster.

Punter, J. (1990, October). The ten commandments of architecture and urban design. *The Planner, 76*(39), 10-14.

Randall, G. & Brown, S. (1999). Prevention is better than cure: New solutions to street homelessness from Crisis. London: Crisis.

Raising the Roof. (2001). *From street to stability: A compilation of findings on the paths to homelessness and its prevention*. Retrieved on October 15, 2006 from http://www.raisingtheroof.org/ss-reso-index.cfm#b

Relph, E. (1987). *The modern urban landscape*. London: Croom Helm.

Renshaw, K. D. (2007). Perceived criticism only matters when it comes from those you live with. *Journal of Clinical Psychology, 63*(12), 1171-9.

Resnick, H. & Jaffee, B. (1982). The physical environment and social welfare. *Social Casework, 63*(6), 354-362.

Riga, A. (2008, February 25). Denis Lazure, 1925-2008. Parti Quebecois's champion of mental patients' rights. *Montreal Gazette*, A6.

Riger, S. & Lavrakas, P. J. (1981). Community ties: Patterns of attachment and social interaction in urban neighborhoods. *American Journal of Community Psychology, 9*, 55-66.

Rose, A. (1958). *Regent Park: A study in slum clearance*. Toronto: University of Toronto Press.

Rose, D. (2004). Discourses and experiences of social mix in gentrifying neighborhoods: A Montreal case study. *Canadian Journal of Urban Research, 32*(2), 278-316.

Rosenthal, R. (2000). Imaging homelessness and homeless people: Visions and strategies within the movement. *Journal of Social Distress and the Homeless, 9*(2), 111-126.

Rothman, D. J. (1971). *The discovery of the asylum: Social order and disorder in the new republic*. Boston: Little, Brown and Company.

Rowe, S. & Wolch, J. (1990). Social networks in time and space: Homeless women in skid row, Los Angeles. *Annals of the Association of American Geographers, 80*(2), 184-204.

Rybczynski, W. (1987). *Home: A short history of an idea*. New York: Penguin Books.

Sandalack, B. A. & Nicolai A. (1998). *Urban structure Halifax: An urban design approach*. Halifax: TUNS Press.

Sandalack, B. A. & Nicolai A. (2006). *The Calgary project: Urban form/urban life*. Calgary: University of Calgary Press.

Saunders, P. & Williams, P. (1988). The constitution of the home: Towards a research agenda. *Housing Studies, 3*(2), 81-93.

Sennett, R. (1969). *Classic essays on the cultures of cities*. New York: Appleton-Century- Crofts.

Sennett, R. (1970a). *Families against the city*. Cambridge, MA: Harvard University Press.

Sennett, R. (1970b). *The uses of disorder*. New York: Vintage.

Shier, M., Walsh, C. A., & Graham, J. R. (2007). Conceptualizing optimum homeless shelter service delivery: The interconnection between programming, community, and the built environment. *Canadian Journal of Urban Research, 16*(1), 1-18.

Shlay, A. B. & Rossi, P. H. (1992). Social science research and contemporary studies of homelessness. *Annual Review of Sociology*, 18, 129-160.

Sibley, D. (1995). *Geographies of exclusion*. New York: Routledge.

Simon, H. (1996). Municipal regulation of the homeless in public spaces. In J. Baumohl (Ed.), *Homelessness in America* (pp. 149-159). Phoenix, AZ.: The Oryx Press.

Sixsmith, J. (1986). The meaning of home: An exploratory study of environmental experience. *Journal of Environmental Psychology*, 6, 281-98.

Skjaeveland, O., Garling, T., & Maeland, J. G. (1996). A multidimensional measure of neighboring. *American Journal of Community Psychology, 24*(3), 413-436.

Smith, M. P. & Peters, B. G. (1987). The uses of neighborhood revitalization. In C. S. Yadav (Ed.), *Perspectives in urban geography: Slums, urban decline and revitalization*, (pp. 109-121). New Delhi: Concept Publishing Company.

Smith, N. (1996). *The new urban frontier: Gentrification and the revanchist city*. London: Routledge.

Snow, D. A. & Anderson, L. (1993). *Down on their luck: A study of homeless street people*. Berkeley: University of California Press.

Soja, E. (2000). *Postmetropolis*. New York: Blackwell Publishing.

Statistics Canada (2005). *Censuses of population*, 1851 - 2001. Retrieved May 27, 2008 from http://www40.statcan.ca/l01/cst01/demo62a.htm

Statistics Canada (2008). *Censuses of population*. Retrieved May 27, 2008 from http://www45.statcan.gc.ca/2008/cgco_2008_001b-eng.htm

Sumka, H. J. (1979). Neighborhood revitalization and displacement. *American Planning Association Journal, 45*, 480-487.

Takahashi, L. (1998). *Homelessness, aids, and stigmatization: The NIMBY syndrome in the United States at the end of the twentieth century.* Oxford: Clarendon Press.

Taylor, I. (1996). Fear and crime, urban fortunes and suburban social movements. *Sociology, 30*, 317-337.

Taylor, R. B. & Brower, S. (1985). Home and near-home territories. In D. W. Meinig (Ed.), *The interpretation of ordinary landscape* (pp. 183-212). New York: Plenum.

Thompson, D. (1961). *On growth and form*. London: Cambridge University Press.

Tognoli, J. & Howritz, J. (1982). From childhood to adult home: Environmental transformation. In P. Bart, A. Chen & G. Francescato (Eds.), *Knowledge for design; EDRA 13 proceedings* (pp. 321-328). Washington: Environmental Design Research Association.

Trancik, R. (1986). *Finding lost space: Theories of urban design*. New York: Van Nostrand Reinhold.

Turagabeci, A. R., Nakamura, K., Kizuki, M., & Takano, T. (2007). Family structure and health, how companionship acts as a buffer against ill health. *Health and Quality of Life Outcomes, 5*(1), 61-70.

Unger, D. G. & Wandersman, A. (1982). Neighboring in an urban environment. *American Journal of Community Psychology, 10*, 493-509.

UN General Assembly. (1948). *Universal declaration of human rights*. Retrieved June 5, 2008, from http://www.un.org/Overview/rights.html

van den Berg, L., van der Meer, J., & Pol, P. M. J. (2003). Organising capacity and social policies in European cities. *Urban Studies, 40*(10), 1959-1978.

Veness, A. (1994). Designer shelters as models and makers of home: New responses of homelessness in urban America. *Urban Geography, 15*, 150-167

Vergara, C. (1995). *The new American ghetto*. New Jersey: Rutgers University Press

von Mahs, J. (2005). The socio-spatial exclusion of single homeless people in Berlin and Los Angeles. *American Behavioral Scientist, 48*(8), 928-960.

Vidler, A. (1996). *Architecture after history: Nostalgia and modernity at the end of the century*. London: RIBA Annual Discourse.

Vitale, A. S. (2008). *City of disorder: How the quality of life campaign transformed New York politics*. New York: New York University Press.

Wacquant, C. (1999). Urban marginality in the coming millennium. *Urban Studies, 36*, 1639-1647.

Wagner, D. (1993). *Checkerboard square: Culture and resistance in a homeless community*. Boulder: Westview Press.

Wallis, M. A. & Kwok S. (Eds.). (2008). *Daily struggles: The deepening racialization and feminization of poverty in Canada*. Toronto: Canadian Scholars' Press.

Walsh, C. A., Graham, J. R., & Shier, M. (in press). Towards a common goal: A holistic perspective in determining "best practices" for homeless shelter service delivery. *Social Development Issues*.

Walsh, C. A., Rutherford, G., & Kuzmak, N. (in press). Characteristics of home: Perspectives of women who are homeless. *The Qualitative Report*.

Walz, T., Willenbring, G., & Demoil, L. (1974). Environmental design. *Social Work, 19*(1), 38-46.

Weeks, W. (2004). Creating attractive services which citizens want to attend. *Australian Social Work, 57*(4), 319-330.

Werner, C. M. (1987). Home interiors: A time and place for interpersonal relationships. *Environment and Behavior, 19*(2), 169-79.

Winchester, H. P. M. & Costello, L. N. (1995). Living on the street: Social organization and gender relations of Australian street kids. *Environmental Planning, Society and Space, 13*, 329-348.

Wright, G. (1980). *Moralism and the model home: Domestic architecture and cultural conflict in Chicago*. Chicago: University of Chicago Press.

Wolch, J. & Dear, M. (1993). *Malign neglect*. San Francisco: Journey-Bass

Worpole, K. (2000). *Here comes the sun: Architecture and public space in twentieth century European culture*. London: Reaktion Books.

Yanetta, A. & Third, H. (1999). *Homelessness in Scotland: A good practice note*. Edinburgh: Chartered Institute of Housing in Scotland.